# WINNING WITH STRATEGY

# WINNING WITH STRATEGY

A GAME CHANGING APPROACH TO STRATEGY
THAT WORKS

Robert J. Frost

Copyright © **Robert Frost 2025**

WINNING WITH STRATEGY™

Library of Congress Cataloging-in-Publication Data

Library of Congress Control Number: 2025919554

Paperback ISBN: 979-8-9930622-1-1

Hardback ISBN: 979-8-9930622-0-4

eBook ISBN: 979-8-9930622-2-8

First Trade Publication September 2025

All Rights Reserved. Any unauthorized reprint or use of this material is strictly prohibited. No part of this book may be reproduced or transmitted in any form or by any means, electronic or mechanical, including photocopying, recording, or by any information storage and retrieval system without express written permission from the author.

All reasonable attempts have been made to verify the accuracy of the information provided in this publication. Nevertheless, the author assumes no responsibility for any errors and/or omissions.

# Dedication

*"All your dreams come true if you have the courage to pursue them."*— *Walt Disney*

To my greatest inspiration for winning—
my incredible wife, Noel, and our amazing children,
Kaitlyn, Kayleigh, and Hunter.

Everything I am, and everything I ever hope to be,
is because of your unwavering love, encouragement, and belief in me.

This book is for you.

Keep pursuing your dreams.

## Praise for WINNING WITH STRATEGY

"In an era marked by rapid market shifts and relentless competition, 'Winning with Strategy' offers a timely and indispensable guide for businesses striving not just to survive, but to truly thrive. This book moves beyond mere buzzwords, delivering a practical and actionable framework for developing game-changing strategies that deliver tangible results." *David Woodworth, President of Terillium*

"*Winning with Strategy* is a powerful blend of practical frameworks and insight that shows leaders how to turn vision into results. Robert Frost distills two decades of experience with Fortune 500 companies and startups into a repeatable process that anyone can apply - in the boardroom and in personal goals. What makes this book stand out is its focus on people and that trust and alignment drive real change. Inspiring, actionable, and energizing, this book will help you not only build strategy - but win with it."
*Karl W. Einolf, Ph.D. President at Indiana Tech*

"Having experienced many business transformations across more than 10 different companies, I kept thinking I wish I had read this book 25 years ago! It not only provides a recipe for success and roadmap for winning but also a 'jump start' for anyone just starting their careers who may be puzzled by why there are so many failures out there."
*James Canigur, VP of IT at Binks*

"Effective strategy requires an actionable framework, not just vision, as this book clarifies. Each element of Robert's approach is crucial for creating meaningful change and sustaining growth. The book provided a career-defining model. It's a must-read for anyone committed to leading transformation and long-term success."
*Kelsey Schenk, Senior Change Management Professional at Salesforce*

# Preface

The morning after I submitted the final manuscript for this book, I went kayaking with my wife Noel on Dallas Lake in Northeast Indiana, where we live. As the sun rose over the still water, I found myself reflecting on why I wrote this book—and imagining how different my journey might have been if I had this information when I was just starting my career.

Over the past two decades, I've had the privilege of developing strategy and leading transformational initiatives at some of the world's most respected companies. I've worked alongside exceptional leaders and mentors, and while there were certainly challenges along the way—lessons learned the hard way—I'm deeply grateful for the experiences that shaped my perspective.

This book is the product of those experiences: a practical, proven framework for achieving meaningful goals through strategic thinking. It's a guide not only to building strategy—but to winning with it.

Although the insights in these pages will absolutely serve business leaders, this book isn't just for the boardroom. It's for individuals striving toward their personal dreams. For schools working to shape the next generation. For healthcare providers saving lives. For nonprofits creating lasting impact. The principles of great strategy apply wherever people are reaching for something better.

Because in the end, this book is as much about winning as it is about strategy. With the right strategy, you can accomplish anything. And let's face it—life's a lot more fun when you're winning.

Robert J. Frost

Dallas Lake, LaGrange County, Indiana

July 2025

**Author's Note:** The real-world stories in this book are drawn from actual experiences and are intended solely for illustrative purposes. Certain details have been modified to protect confidentiality and enhance clarity.

# Table of Contents

Dedication .................................................................. i

Preface ..................................................................... ii

Chapter 1 On Becoming A Winner ............................. 1

Chapter 2 Focus ....................................................... 15
*Keep Your Target in Your Sights*

Chapter 3 Relationships ........................................... 32
*Build Trust to Drive Alignment and Change*

Chapter 4 Ownership ............................................... 46
*Create a Culture of Accountability*

Chapter 5 Strategy ................................................... 59
*Choose the Right How*

Chapter 6 Tactics ..................................................... 67
*Execute with Discipline*

Chapter 7 Bringing It All Together ........................... 75
*From Process to Action*

Chapter 8 Strategy Realization ................................. 83
*Make Winning the Only Option*

Chapter 9 A Passion For Winning ........................... 102

Chapter 10 Make Winning Your Habit .................... 114

Appendix ............................................................... 120
*How to Use the Strategic Planning Canvas*

About The Author .................................................. 129

# Chapter 1

# On Becoming a Winner

*"The will to win is not nearly as important as the will to prepare to win."*
— *Bobby Knight*

**Strategy is about winning.**

You can accomplish anything with the right strategy. So why are most people, and most organizations, not good at strategy or winning?

Everyone wants to win. But wanting to win isn't what separates the best from the rest—*preparing* to win is. That's where strategy comes in.

The most successful people and organizations don't rely on luck, talent alone, or bursts of inspiration. They succeed because they build a clear strategy, align their people and resources, and execute with discipline. They don't just react—they prepare. They don't just move fast—they move with purpose.

This book is about that preparation. It's about closing the gap between vision and results, between intention and action. It's about winning—deliberately, consistently, and with clarity—through strategy.

According to The Strategy Institute, strategy in its broadest sense is the means by which individuals or organizations achieve their objectives. In this book, a *winning strategy* goes beyond simply defining the "how." It integrates the *what*, the *why*, the *who*, and the *how*—aligning purpose, people, and culture with clear strategies and actionable plans to drive successful execution and meaningful results. Many people, including experienced business leaders, struggle with strategy. They may have clear goals and ambitious plans, but often lack a practical way to turn those goals into real, lasting results. They have not learned how to approach strategy as a reliable, repeatable process.

I saw this unfold during a session with a CEO and his senior leadership team. The topic was business transformation. A consultant asked a straightforward question: "What's your long-term strategy?" Silence followed. After an awkward pause, one executive finally replied, "We can't predict the future," and began listing company objectives. In that moment, it became clear. They did not have a strategy. They had hopes, not direction.

This scenario is more common than most people realize. Research shows that 90 percent of organizations fail to execute their strategies. Nine out of ten startups do not survive. Each year, around 30,000 new products are launched, and 95 percent fail. Individuals face similar challenges. By February, 80 percent of New Year's resolutions have already been abandoned, most without ever getting a fair attempt.

These numbers highlight something important. The hardest part is not setting goals. It is following through. There is a wide gap between what we intend to do and what actually gets done. What separates those who succeed is the ability to commit to a future vision and take consistent steps to bring it to life.

In his article *Killer Strategies*, Gary Hamel put it bluntly: "The dirty little secret of the strategy industry is that it doesn't have any theory of strategy creation." He was right. Most organizations—and most individuals—begin with goals, not strategy. They focus on execution without first answering the question: *execute what, and why?* But the best organizations know the truth. Greatness requires both great strategy and great execution. One without the other doesn't work. Flawless execution of a flawed strategy still leads you off a cliff. And the best strategy in the world is meaningless if you can't bring it to life.

Over the course of my career, I've had the opportunity to both develop and execute strategy across a wide range of organizations—from small, private equity-backed startups to mid-market growth companies to global Fortune 500 leaders. Along the way, I've learned what works, what doesn't, and—most importantly—*why*. Those experiences led to the development of a repeatable process, one that works regardless of company size, industry, or context. It applies at every level: corporate strategy, business unit strategy, departmental plans, major initiatives, and even personal strategy for achieving life goals.

If you have something meaningful you want to achieve, this book is for you. It's not another treatise on market analysis, SWOT grids, or environmental scans—though it will help you improve those, too. This is a book about how to win with strategy—*real* strategy—no matter what game you're playing.

This is the book I wish I had when I was starting out. It's written to share the lessons I've learned—so you can avoid some of the costly trial and error that comes with learning the hard way.

This book also introduces two powerful tools for winning with strategy: the **FROST Strategy Pyramid™** and the **FROST Strategic Planning Canvas**—a one-page summary that brings everything together to guide clear, focused strategic planning and realization. The remainder of this introduction offers a high-level overview of these frameworks and how they help turn purpose into progress.

This framework goes beyond traditional strategic planning and execution. It's an end-to-end process that begins with a clear focus on *what* you're doing and *why*. It also integrates the human side of change, drawing on Prosci® best practices in change management and insights from Nobel Prize-winning research in behavioral economics.

These foundational elements are essential to bridging the gap between strategy and execution. When you get the focus, the team, and the culture right, your strategies aren't just more likely to succeed—they're *seven times* more likely to deliver results.

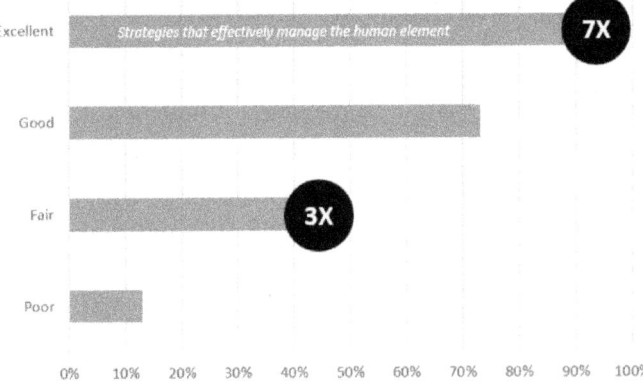

**Effectively Managing the People Side of Strategy Increases Success Rates by 700%**

Source: Research Hub ©2023 Prosci, Inc.

## Strategy That Moves People

Strategy, at its core, is about change. But here's the truth: organizations don't change—people do.

And yet, in most conversations about strategy, we rush straight to execution. We talk about goals, initiatives, timelines, and metrics. We lay out roadmaps and build Gantt charts. However, we miss the most important variable in the equation: the people who will bring the strategy to life.

That's the hidden gap. Not a failure of planning, but a failure to connect strategy to *human behavior*. The real challenge isn't crafting a plan—it's getting people to change what they do.

### The Missing Link: People Don't Commit with Logic Alone

Nobel laureate and Carnegie Mellon professor Herbert Simon, in his *Theory of Bounded Rationality*, helped the world understand that people don't make decisions based on logic alone. Emotions are not the opposite of rationality—they're another form of it. Emotions, he showed, are part of how we think.

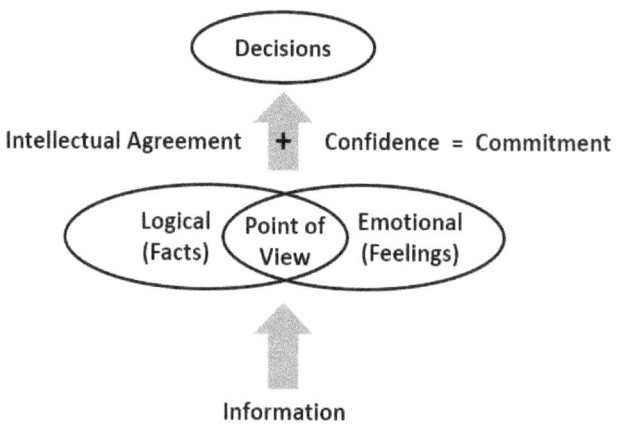

**Theory of Bounded Rationality**

Source: The PAR Group ©2007

Daniel Kahneman expanded on this in *Thinking, Fast and Slow*, revealing that decisions are driven by both fast, emotional instincts and slower, logical reasoning. This is why getting someone to agree with a strategy on paper isn't enough. Intellectual agreement isn't the same as personal commitment.

You can convince someone with facts, but if you haven't moved how they *feel* about those facts, you haven't moved them at all.

I first began to grasp the real power of the human element in strategic decision-making while working alongside **Dave Matheson**, President and CEO of **SmartOrg** and co-author of *The Smart Organization*. A respected voice in portfolio management and strategic thinking, Dave and I partnered during our time at Zimmer Biomet to implement value-based management across our European locations. That experience shaped my strategic philosophy in lasting ways.

What stood out wasn't just the rigor of models or the strength of data—it was how much the outcome depended on people. Behind every decision were personal beliefs, unspoken biases, and varying levels of willingness to commit. Success didn't come from perfect spreadsheets but from alignment, trust, and shared conviction. Strategy only moves forward when people believe in it.

*"When people commit to a bold goal, when they align with a mission, when they feel part of something meaningful, they change."*

Albert Einstein once said, "Nothing happens until something moves." In strategy, that movement starts when people shift their behavior. And that shift doesn't come from mandates or plans alone—it comes from personal choice. True change happens when people decide, deep down, that it matters.

And that decision? It isn't just intellectual. It's deeply human. It comes from the heart as much as the head.

### The Heart of Strategy Is the Human Heart

This is the overlooked truth in most strategic playbooks: transformation isn't just organizational—it's *personal*. When people commit to a bold goal, when they align with a mission, when they feel part of something meaningful, they change. And that change is what makes real transformation possible.

But you cannot achieve that with logic alone. You have to move people—**hearts and minds together.**

### A Framework That Honors Both Sides

Most strategy models emphasize the logical side of execution: if we complete these tactics, we achieve these strategies; if we hit these strategies, we hit the objective.

That's necessary—but it's not sufficient.

The **FROST Strategy Pyramid™** framework (see image below) is built differently. It integrates both the *logical* and the *emotional* sides of change.

- The foundation—**Focus, Relationships, and Ownership**—speaks directly to the *human* side of transformation. It aligns people to purpose, builds trust and commitment, and creates a culture where accountability is real.
- The core layers—**Strategy and Tactics**—provide the logical path to execution. They convert vision into action, and action into results.

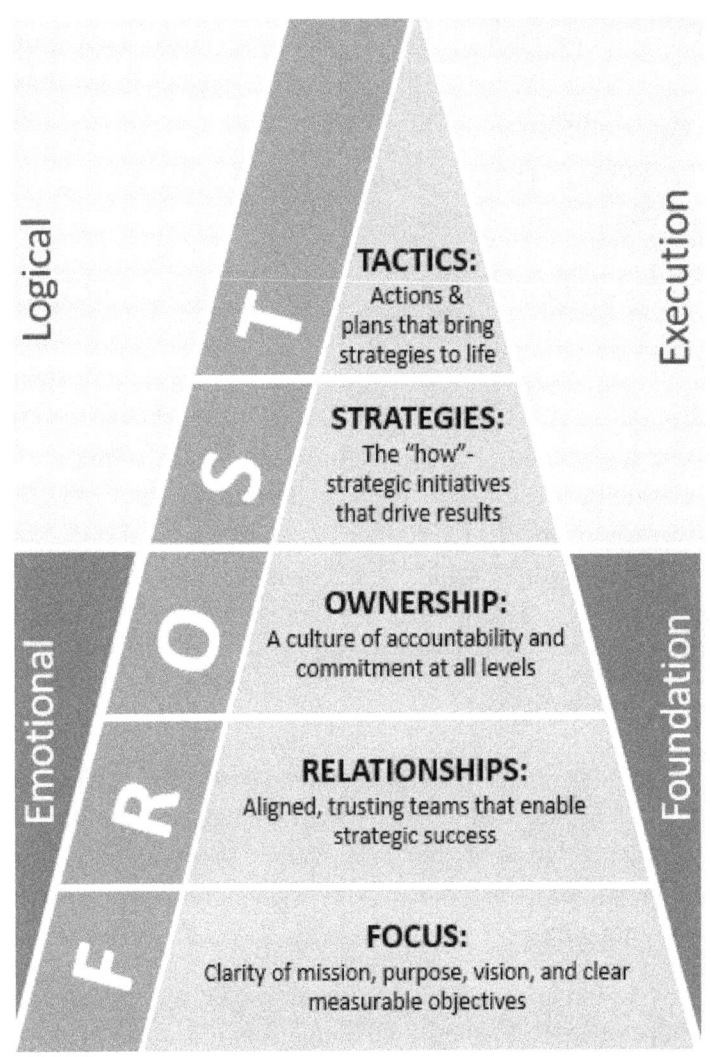

The FROST Strategy Pyramid™

When both sides are engaged—when hearts are aligned and plans are clear—strategy moves faster. Execution becomes easier. Change becomes possible.

That's what this framework is designed to do. And that's the shift that changes everything.

**FOCUS**

A great strategy starts with disciplined focus. Focus brings clarity of purpose and alignment. It begins with your *mission*—what you're doing—and your *purpose*—why you're doing it. From there, you define your *vision*, a vivid and inspiring picture of what success looks like, followed by an honest assessment of your *current state*. Only then do you set clear, measurable *objectives*—the non-negotiable outcomes required to realize your vision. Without focus, effort diffuses. With it, energy aligns.

**RELATIONSHIPS**

Strategy only moves when people do. Behind every plan that works is a team that believes in what they're building and feels connected to its purpose. When people are aligned, motivated, and trusted, the work carries more weight and more meaning.

Trust is what turns a group into a team. It grows through day-to-day consistency, shared challenges, and a sense of safety that allows people to speak honestly and take ownership. It's what allows strategy to hold together under pressure. When trust is strong, people move with clarity. They're faster to adapt, quicker to support each other, and more grounded in the bigger picture.

## OWNERSHIP

A culture of ownership turns strategy into results. From the CEO to the front lines, everyone must take personal responsibility for the outcome. Ownership means alignment, commitment, and a shared sense of accountability. It means no excuses, no blame—just a relentless focus on delivering what matters. Without ownership, strategy stalls. With it, momentum builds.

## STRATEGIES

Strategies are the *how*—the high-leverage initiatives that drive results. Each strategy is designed to move one or more key objectives forward. They are the major programs, priorities, or change efforts that shape the future.

## TACTICS

Tactics are where strategy hits the ground. These specific actions, plans, and tasks bring each strategy to life. Thoughtfully chosen and rigorously executed, tactics turn vision into progress.

The gap between strategy and execution isn't just a corporate problem—it's a universal one. It affects anyone who wants to achieve something meaningful. The remainder of this book dives into each framework element and shows how it applies across all contexts: business enterprises, healthcare systems, schools, nonprofits, even personal goals and lifelong dreams. My hope is that *Winning with Strategy* becomes as practical and powerful for you as it has been for me—across work, life, and everything in between.

Whether you're leading a company, guiding a team, serving a community, or pursuing a personal goal, this framework is designed to help you win—with clarity, with purpose, and with discipline.

Strategy isn't just for executives in corner offices. It's for anyone who's serious about achieving something that matters.

In the chapters ahead, we'll take a deeper dive into the key ingredients of winning with strategy—and how you can apply them to create lasting results.

It all starts with **Focus.** Let's begin.

Chapter 1 Summary

- **Winning isn't luck—it's built.** Success comes not from talent or inspiration alone, but from preparing to win through disciplined strategy.

- **Strategy is the bridge between vision and execution.** It closes the gap between intention and results, turning goals into reality.

- **Most people and organizations struggle with strategy.** They set goals but lack a repeatable process to achieve them—leading to high failure rates in business initiatives, product launches, and even personal resolutions.

- **A winning strategy goes beyond "how."** It integrates the *what*, *why*, *who*, and *how*—aligning purpose, people, and culture with actionable plans.

- **Great strategy requires both design and execution.** Flawless execution of a flawed strategy fails; a brilliant strategy without execution is wasted. Both are essential.

- **People are the missing link.** Strategy isn't just logic on paper—it moves only when people believe, commit, and change their behavior.

- **The human side of strategy matters.** Emotions drive decisions as much as logic; true commitment comes from aligning hearts and minds, not just tasks and metrics.

- **The FROST Strategy Pyramid™** provides an integrated framework that honors both logic and emotion:
    - *Focus* – clarity of mission, purpose, vision, and objectives.
    - *Relationships* – trust and alignment that turn groups into teams.
    - *Ownership* – accountability and commitment across all levels.
    - *Strategies* – the high-leverage "how" that drives progress.
    - *Tactics* – the concrete actions that bring strategies to life.

- **This is a universal framework.** Whether in business, education, healthcare, nonprofits, or personal goals, the process works—because strategy is about people, purpose, and disciplined execution.

- **The journey begins with Focus.** Every great strategy starts with clarity—knowing what you're doing, why it matters, and where you stand today.

## Chapter 2

## Focus

Keep Your Target in Your Sights

*"Where there is no vision, the people perish."*
— *Proverbs 29:18*

Knowing where you're going matters more than how fast you move. It means that every meaningful strategy begins with focus.

Across industries, across stages of business, I've seen the same pattern repeat itself. In boardrooms with experienced executives and in conversations with first-time founders, people often rush straight into action. They start building plans, launching projects, and chasing results, without first pausing to ask the essential questions. What are we trying to do? Why does it matter? What will success actually look like?

Without that clarity, even the most talented teams lose direction. Great ideas lose momentum. But when focus comes first, everything starts to align. Energy becomes purposeful. Resources flow where they're needed most. And strategy gains the traction it needs to move forward. This chapter begins with Focus, the first and most foundational element of winning with strategy.

For organizations and individuals that consistently outperform, clarity isn't a luxury—it's a prerequisite. They begin by answering four essential questions:

1. **What are we doing?** *(Mission)*
   What is the core work, the reason this organization, project, or individual exists? Mission defines the *what*, and it should be clear, specific, and actionable.
2. **Why are we doing it?** *(Purpose)*
   Purpose goes deeper. It's the higher cause and emotional driver that gives work meaning. Without a compelling "why," even well-designed strategies lose steam.
3. **What does success look like?** *(Vision)*
   Vision paints a compelling picture of the destination. It's concrete, not abstract. It gives teams something they can see, believe in, and rally behind.
4. **Where are we today?** *(Current State)*
   Strategy can't begin until you're honest about your starting point. That means clear-eyed assessments of capabilities, performance, and gaps.

Only after answering those questions can you define your **Objectives**—the hard, measurable outcomes that bridge today's reality and tomorrow's vision. These objectives become the foundation for strategy, the yardstick for progress, and the basis for accountability.

When organizations skip these steps, they lose alignment and momentum. Teams pull in different directions, leaders chase too many priorities, and execution becomes reactive. But when clarity is established—when the mission, purpose, vision, and objectives are clearly defined—focus becomes a force multiplier.

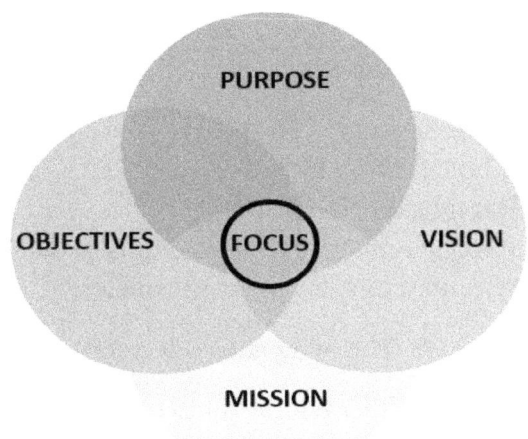

## Mission: Define What You're Doing

Great strategy begins with a clear understanding of *what* you are here to do.

Your **mission** defines the core of your work. It's not a slogan, and it's not a marketing line—it's a declaration of intent. It tells your team, your stakeholders, and yourself exactly *what* you are trying to accomplish in the most fundamental terms.

In organizations that win consistently, the mission is sharp, specific, and deeply understood. It acts as a filter: when new ideas surface or priorities compete, the mission helps you decide what fits—and what doesn't.

Most failing strategies begin with ambiguity. A mission that is too broad, too generic, or too vague opens the door to misalignment. Teams pull in different directions. Energy is scattered. Progress stalls.

*"When clarity is established—when the mission, purpose, vision, and objectives are clearly defined—focus becomes a force multiplier."*

Compare the difference:

- **Vague mission:** "To be the best in the industry."
- **Clear mission:** "To deliver affordable, minimally invasive orthopedic solutions that restore mobility for aging patients."

One is forgettable. The other guides decisions.

The mission doesn't have to be long. In fact, the best ones rarely are. But it must be *clear*. It should tell you what game you're playing—and what winning looks like at the most fundamental level.

### A Litmus Test for a Great Mission

Ask yourself:

- Can every person on the team explain it in their own words?
- Does it rule some things *out*, not just invite everything in?
- Does it help prioritize resources, time, and attention?

If the answer to any of these is "no," it's time to sharpen it.

## Mission in Action: Zimmer Biomet

Few leaders embody a passion for winning, such as **Ivan Tornos**, president and CEO of **Zimmer Biomet**. His energy, focus, and commitment to excellence helped create a mission-driven culture that reached every corner of the organization. Under his leadership, winning was not just a goal. It became a mindset that people believed in and carried forward every day.

At Zimmer Biomet, the mission was never just words on a wall. It was a shared belief, expressed through the actions of every team and every leader.

**"To alleviate pain and improve the quality of life for people around the world."**

That was our mission. And our CEO made sure we never lost sight of it.

He regularly hosted mission ceremonies, gatherings that brought together every level of the organization, from executives to factory workers. Each person received a medal engraved with our mission. It was a small gesture, but one that held deep meaning.

We listened to stories from patients whose lives had been changed by our work. We heard from nurses and surgeons who used our products to help people heal. And we listened to leaders who spoke not just about revenue, but about impact. These ceremonies were moments of clarity and connection.

In those moments, you did not just hear the mission. You felt it.

Later, when it came time to make tough decisions about strategy or priorities, those shared moments made alignment easier. We were not just building orthopedic devices. We were restoring movement, dignity, and freedom. That sense of purpose created commitment. And that commitment translated into action.

I saw a similar energy at Sofamor Danek, the orthopedic spine company I worked at for nearly a decade before it was acquired by Medtronic. Bill George, Medtronic's former CEO, once said, "In mission-driven companies, employee motivation comes from believing in the purpose of the work and being part of something worthwhile." That rang true. At Sofamor Danek, purpose was not just a slogan. It was the force that united us and moved us forward.

The best organizations do not just define their mission. They live it. And when that happens, strategy becomes more than a plan. It becomes something worth fighting for.

**Purpose: Define Why You're Doing It**

If mission defines what you do, **purpose** defines *why* it matters.

Purpose is the emotional force behind strategy. It transforms a plan into something people believe in, and a group of individuals into a united team. Mission provides direction. Purpose provides meaning—and meaning is what sustains commitment when the work becomes difficult.

In organizations that succeed over the long term, purpose functions as a strategic anchor. It attracts people who share your values, helps keep them aligned, and builds a level of commitment that performance incentives alone cannot create.

When people are connected to the "why," they show up differently. They bring energy, accountability, and resilience. They stay longer, speak up sooner, and step forward when challenges arise—not out of obligation, but because they care.

This isn't just anecdotal. Research consistently shows that purpose-driven companies lead in employee engagement, customer loyalty, and long-term financial performance. Purpose clarifies what matters most, especially when decisions fall into the gray areas where policies don't provide clear answers.

Without a deeper reason behind the work, strategies stall. Teams lose momentum. But with purpose, even the hardest tasks become worthwhile.

**To uncover that deeper reason, ask:**

- What change are we trying to create—for our industry, our community, or the world?
- Why does this work matter—beyond revenue or growth?
- Who stands to benefit when our mission is fulfilled?

At Zimmer Biomet, the mission was to alleviate pain and improve quality of life. But what truly united people was the deeper purpose behind it—the vision of someone walking again, working again, living again. You can see this in the stories shared at mission ceremonies and the pride employees take in their work each day.

Purpose does more than inspire. It aligns people around something meaningful. And when that happens, strategy moves forward with clarity, conviction, and power.

### The Power of Purpose: A Personal Example

A few years ago, I set a goal to lose weight. I had a clear plan: eat healthier and exercise consistently. I outlined specific steps like counting calories, tracking my meals, and committing to a workout schedule. On paper, everything looked right.

But I struggled to follow through. After a long day at work, I'd skip the gym and reach for something quick and unhealthy. I kept telling myself I'd start over tomorrow. The problem wasn't a lack of knowledge. I knew exactly what to do. I just wasn't doing it.

One morning, looking in the mirror, I asked myself a different question. Why do I really want this?

The answer had nothing to do with the number on the scale. I wanted the energy to keep up with my kids. I wanted to come home from work and be fully present with my wife and family. I wanted to lead by example and live the discipline I talked about—not just preach it.

That shift changed everything. When I had to choose between a healthy meal and fast food, I thought about being there for my family, not just about nutrition. When my alarm rang before sunrise, it wasn't just about checking off a workout. It was about building the life I wanted to lead.

The strategy stayed the same. The tactics didn't change. But once I connected to something more meaningful, my commitment became real. Purpose gave my choices weight. It gave me a reason to follow through, even when it wasn't easy.

That's the difference purpose makes. It turns effort into conviction and gives you something to lean on when willpower wears thin.

## Vision: Define What Success Looks Like

If mission is *what* you do and purpose is *why* it matters, then **vision** is *where you're going*.

A clear, compelling vision paints a picture of the future you're working to create. It's not about vague aspirations or generic targets. Vision is specific. Tangible. It should allow people to see themselves in it—and move toward it with energy.

Vision gives strategy direction. It translates purpose into possibility. Without it, teams drift. They may work hard, even heroically—but without a common destination, effort gets fragmented and momentum fades.

A strong vision answers three core questions:

- What will success look like when we've fulfilled our mission?
- How will the world, our organization, or ourselves be different?
- What future are we inviting people to help create?

Consider the difference:

- **Vague vision:** "To be a market leader through innovation and excellence."
- **Clear vision:** "By 2028, to restore mobility to 5 million patients annually, expand access to care in underserved regions, and set the global standard in orthopedic outcomes."

One is generic. The other provides focus, direction, and urgency.

Great leaders don't just craft a vision—they *define* it. They make it measurable. They turn the abstract into something people can act on. And they repeat it often—until it becomes a shared lens through which every decision is made.

## The Power of Vision—And Visualization

Every meaningful journey starts with a clear picture of where you're going. Great leaders don't just set goals, they see them. They form a mental image so vivid it begins to influence how they think, how they lead, and how others respond. That clarity becomes a quiet but steady force, guiding each decision and shaping every step forward.

I first learned about the power of visualization early in my career. Reading *Think and Grow Rich* by Napoleon Hill opened my eyes to how leaders like Andrew Carnegie mentally rehearsed success before ever achieving it. That idea stuck with me. Over time, I came across more voices, like Rhonda Byrne and John Assaraf, who showed how mental focus can create real momentum. What began as an idea became a habit.

And it's not just theory. Neuroscience confirms what many of us have experienced: when you imagine something vividly and consistently, your brain responds as if it's already happening. It activates the same pathways, builds familiarity, and creates a kind of mental muscle memory. It prepares you to act with more confidence when the moment finally arrives.

In my own life, visualization has been a steady companion. Before leading large teams, I spent time picturing the kind of leader I wanted to be. Before building a business, I imagined what it would take—and what it would feel like, to bring it to life. That mental clarity helped me move through uncertainty with more conviction.

A clear vision, reinforced through consistent practice, does more than motivate—it creates alignment. It helps you stay grounded, especially when challenges arise. And over time, what once lived only in your mind begins to show up in your reality.

**A Vision Worth Following**

Vision is where many leaders stumble. They think it's "fluff" or abstract. But a compelling vision becomes a rallying cry. It invites commitment. It energizes culture. And it forces clarity when trade-offs inevitably arise.

Strategy is about closing the gap between *where you are* and *where you want to be*. That means you need both ends of the bridge—your current reality and your vision for the future.

And that brings us to the next step: taking a hard, honest look at where things stand today.

**Current State: Know Where You Stand**

You can't build a bridge without knowing where you're starting from.

Once you've defined your mission, purpose, and vision, the next step is to confront reality. That means getting clear on your **current state**—the unvarnished truth about where things stand today.

This is a challenge for many leaders. They skip the hard questions. They rely on surface-level metrics or inflated narratives. But great strategy demands a clear-eyed assessment of reality—*not as you wish it were, but as it is.*

Jim Collins called this "confronting the brutal facts." Without that honesty, strategy becomes fantasy. Execution drifts. Teams chase unrealistic goals or underestimate the effort required.

**A Strong Current State Assessment Includes:**

- **Performance metrics:**
  Where are we hitting the mark? Where are we falling short?
- **Capabilities and gaps:**
  What are our core strengths? Where are we vulnerable?
- **Cultural realities:**
  What beliefs, habits, or norms are helping—or hindering—execution?
- **External landscape:**
  What market forces, competitor moves, or regulatory shifts are shaping our environment?

At Wolfpack Chassis, part of our strategic rigor came from facing reality with humility. As we grew, we routinely assessed how we were performing—not just in terms of financials, but in quality, delivery, operational efficiency, and customer satisfaction. We didn't just celebrate success—we studied the setbacks. That level of candor helped us build strategies that were grounded, resilient, and achievable.

I saw the importance of understanding the current state firsthand during an ERP transformation program in partnership with Terillium. Brought in to recover a struggling implementation, their team resisted the urge to jump straight into problem-solving. Instead, they paused to listen and assess before offering any solutions.

Rather than assume what had gone wrong, they asked thoughtful, probing questions:

- What were the key issues with the original implementation?
- What measures did you have in place to quantify failure?
- What changes are you making to avoid repeating the same mistakes?
- What does success look like for your ERP implementation?
- What are your primary goals in adopting a new system?

They used these questions to uncover the real story—what was happening across the organization beneath the surface. As Terillium's president, David Woodworth, explained, *"If the client is unable to answer these questions in adequate fashion, it makes me hesitant to get involved—especially if they won't take a step back, reflect on what went wrong, and commit to the changes needed for success."*

Only after building a clear, honest view of the current state— our strengths, gaps, misalignments, and risks—did they begin to shape a path forward. Their structured, disciplined approach reinforced a vital truth:

Successful execution doesn't begin with answers—it begins with understanding. When you know your current state, you don't just hope for change—you plan for it.

### Focus Brings It All Together

When mission, purpose, vision, and current state are clearly defined, strategy gains traction. You now have a focused foundation: a powerful "what," a compelling "why," a shared view of success, and an honest view of the starting point.

That's where objectives come in—the final step in creating focus, and the first step in turning strategy into execution.

### Objectives: Define What You Must Achieve

Once you've defined where you're going and where you're starting from, strategy demands one more thing: **hard, measurable objectives.**

If vision is the destination, then objectives are the mile markers along the journey. They translate aspiration into action. They turn strategy from a story into a scoreboard.

Too many organizations fall short because they stop at vision. They talk about transformation, growth, innovation—but fail to define what *success actually looks like in measurable terms*. Without objectives, teams work hard but struggle to focus. Progress is hard to track, and accountability fades.

### Great Objectives Are SMART:

- **Specific** - Clear enough that everyone knows what's expected.
- **Measurable** - Quantified with metrics or outcomes.

- **Aligned** - Directly connected to the mission to close the gap between the current state and vision.
- **Realistic** - Achievable based on the resources, time, abilities, and situation.
- **Time-bound** - Anchored to a realistic timeline.

For example:

- **Vague goal:** "Improve customer satisfaction."
- **Clear objective:** "Increase Net Promoter Score from 48 to 60 by Q4."

The difference is night and day. One is open to misinterpretation; the other drives action.

At Wolfpack, our strategic plans were always built around a small set of focused objectives. These weren't just handed down from leadership—they were discussed, debated, and aligned across departments. Everyone knew what we were aiming for. Everyone had a role in achieving it.

And here's the key: we didn't try to do everything. We chose a few high-impact objectives and committed to doing them well. Because focus isn't just about clarity—it's about *discipline*.

**Focus is the First Strategic Advantage**

When you define your mission, your purpose, your vision, your current state, and your objectives, you build the foundation for everything that follows. You gain alignment. You create energy. You filter distractions. And you set the conditions for successful execution.

Strategy begins with focus. Without it, even the best individuals and teams struggle. With it, even the most ambitious goals can be achieved.

Chapter 2 Summary

- **Direction matters more than speed.** Without clarity, even the fastest-moving teams lose momentum and alignment.

- **Strategy begins with focus.** Before action, leaders must pause to ask the essential questions: *What are we doing? Why does it matter? What does success look like? Where are we today?*

- **Clarity drives alignment.** With focus, energy becomes purposeful, resources flow where they're needed, and execution gains traction. Without it, teams scatter and progress stalls.

- **Mission defines the *what*.** A sharp, specific mission acts as a filter, guiding priorities and ensuring alignment.

- **Purpose explains the *why*.** Purpose provides meaning, fuels commitment, and sustains momentum when challenges arise.

- **Vision paints the destination.** A compelling vision makes success tangible and rallying. It transforms aspiration into something people can see and move toward.

- **Current state anchors reality.** Honest assessment of today's capabilities, performance, and gaps prevents strategy from becoming fantasy.

- **Objectives bridge the gap.** SMART objectives translate ambition into measurable outcomes and create accountability.

- **Focus is a force multiplier.** When mission, purpose, vision, current state, and objectives are aligned, strategy shifts from vague aspiration to disciplined execution.

## Chapter 3

## Relationships

Build Trust to Drive Alignment and Change

*"Individual commitment to a group effort - that is what makes a team work, a company work, a society work, a civilization work."*
— *Vince Lombardi*

**People Power Strategy**

No strategy thrives in isolation. Even the most carefully designed plan depends on people to bring it to life. You can have a clear vision and strong objectives, but without a team that's aligned, engaged, and committed, the best ideas stall. Progress slows, and the sense of momentum fades.

Strategy depends on more than logic or structured frameworks. It depends on people, and people are influenced by the strength of their relationships.

**Trust Drives Everything Forward**

At the core of every strong team is trust, a steady belief in each other's intentions, abilities, and integrity. The kind of trust that allows people to speak openly, admit when they're struggling, and challenge ideas with respect.

In demanding, high-pressure environments, trust is the key force that keeps teams grounded and connected. It allows everyone to act quickly and confidently, even in uncertain situations. Trust facilitates swift decision-making, enhances communication, and provides stability when plans change or setbacks occur. Without trust, even the most robust strategies encounter obstacles. Fear can emerge, communication may deteriorate, and teams might start avoiding challenges instead of confronting them directly.

When trust is strong, everything progresses more quickly. Teams feel safe to act, share concerns early, and collaborate to adjust course when necessary. Momentum builds because people are connected, not just to the mission, but also to each other.

**The Leadership Multiplier**

Strong relationships are intentional. Great leaders nurture them through consistency, honesty, and attentive listening. They create space for every voice to matter and understand that real leadership comes from influence, which is built through trust.

When trust flows both ways—when teams feel supported and leaders feel confident in their people—alignment happens naturally. Teams move forward with shared purpose, not out of obligation, but because they believe in the direction and each other.

## Aligning the Team Around Purpose, Mission, and Objectives

Clarity means little without alignment. You can have a compelling mission and a powerful sense of purpose, but if your team doesn't understand it or connect with it, execution falters. Strategy takes shape in the space between what leaders communicate and what teams actually absorb and act upon.

That's why alignment is one of the most important responsibilities of leadership, and one that's often underestimated.

In many organizations, alignment is treated as an annual task. Leaders define objectives and expect departments to follow suit. But often, each team ends up chasing its own version of success, guided by different interpretations of strategy. The result is scattered energy and diluted impact. Alignment isn't about cascading tasks—it's about unifying understanding and commitment at every level.

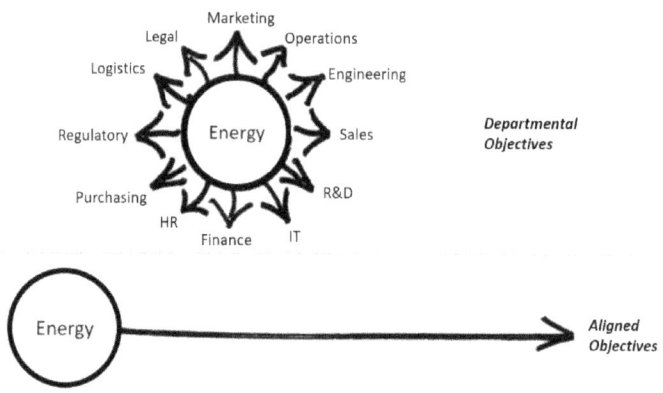

**Departmental vs. Aligned Objectives**

Adapted from Essentialism © 2014 by Greg McKeown

It's perfectly reasonable for departments to have unique strategies and tactics. However, everyone should be aligned around a shared mission and common objectives.

In *The 4 Disciplines of Execution* (McChesney et al.), the authors argue that the true enemy of strategy execution is everyone's day job. Alignment bridges that gap—it connects strategy to the everyday. When people understand how their daily work ladders up to broader goals, strategy becomes real.

And real alignment isn't about compliance—it's about commitment. When teams are aligned, they don't just follow orders; they take ownership. They make smarter decisions because they understand the context. They collaborate more effectively because they're aiming at the same target. And they say no to distractions because they're clear on what truly matters.

> *"Strategy takes shape in the space between what leaders communicate and what teams actually absorb and act upon."*

### From Words to Ownership

At Zimmer Biomet, the mission to alleviate pain and improve lives shaped everything. It influenced how we worked, how we collaborated, and how we understood the impact of our efforts. It gave the work meaning far beyond the walls of the organization.

Every few months, the company held mission ceremonies that brought people together across roles and departments. These gatherings created space to reflect, reconnect, and realign. We heard directly from patients whose lives had changed. We listened to stories from surgeons, caregivers, and frontline staff. The experience made the mission feel tangible. It turned data into people and work into purpose.

That sense of purpose created a steady rhythm, even in difficult moments. When a product launch ran into obstacles or regulatory challenges surfaced, the response wasn't hesitation but focus. Teams stayed engaged, solved problems quickly, and supported one another without needing to be asked. The mission gave people something solid to hold onto, a reason to stay focused, especially when the pressure was real and the path was unclear.

**Questions to Ask as a Leader:**

- Does every person on the team understand the mission and purpose—not just the words, but the *why* behind them?
- Can they describe how their work connects to the larger goals?
- Are we communicating our strategy in ways that resonate at every level of the organization?

Alignment isn't a one-time event. It's a leadership discipline. It requires consistency, storytelling, and intentional communication. But when done well, it transforms strategy from a top-down directive into a shared commitment.

Next, we'll explore the fuel that makes alignment possible: **trust**—and why it starts with vulnerability.

**Building Trust Through Vulnerability and Consistency**

Trust doesn't come from titles. It comes from how you show up.

As a leader, especially in cross-functional environments, you often need to drive outcomes without having formal authority. That's when influence becomes your most valuable tool—and influence only works when it's built on trust.

I've led large, enterprise-wide programs involving hundreds of people—many of whom didn't report to me. I learned quickly that when a transformation fails, it's rarely because the technology was flawed or the strategy was wrong. It's almost always because of people—resistance, misalignment, or fear. Not because people are bad—but because *humans resist change*. That's the starting point. And that's where trust becomes essential.

As a certified Prosci change practitioner, I've come to learn a valuable lesson: while **you can't make people like change, you can help them feel safe enough to embrace it.**

I saw this clearly while leading the development of a Project Management Office (PMO) at International Truck and Engine Corporation. The organization operated in a UAW union environment, and beyond the technical complexities of building a PMO from the ground up, there was a deeper relational challenge; **I had no formal authority over the union leaders.**

I couldn't issue directives or enforce compliance. What I had was the opportunity to lead through influence, and influence begins with building relationships.

Before introducing new processes, I spent time listening. I asked questions, trying to understand what success looked like for them. I learned what they valued, what they feared, and how our plans might affect their people.

Only after those conversations did we shape our PMO goals to reflect outcomes they cared about—job security, growth, and operational excellence. I was transparent about the process and honest about what I didn't yet know. I showed consistency, followed through on my word, and built credibility over time.

The outcome surprised even me. Union leaders didn't just cooperate—they became advocates. They helped promote the PMO across teams. One union president even joked, "You know we're doing half your job for you now, right?"

That partnership helped make the PMO successful, not because it was forced, but because it was owned. It eventually became the standard for project and portfolio management across the organization.

Trust wasn't a bonus or a final add-on. It was the starting point, the steady ground that allowed every step of the process to unfold smoothly. Without it, progress would have stalled. With it, support grew, momentum built, and the work moved forward with confidence.

**Developing the Right Capabilities**

Once the team is aligned and trust is established, the next question is simple—but crucial:

**Can they actually do what the strategy requires?**

Alignment without capability is just good intention. And in high-stakes transformations—whether in business, healthcare, government, or your own personal life—**you can't execute what you're not equipped to do.**

Too often, organizations assume that alignment is enough. That if people understand the mission, they'll figure it out. But great leaders don't make that assumption. They ask the harder question: *Do we have the skills, tools, and capacity to win?*

## Capability is a Leadership Responsibility

Capability-building is not just an HR function or a training task—it's a strategic imperative. Strategy isn't just about choosing the right goals—it's about making sure your team can reach them.

This means:

- **Identifying the capabilities your strategy requires** (e.g., digital fluency, cross-functional collaboration, advanced analytics)
- **Assessing current gaps with honesty** (What can we do today? What are we missing?)
- **Building capacity deliberately** (Hiring, training, reassigning, or upskilling as needed)

It also means building capacity at *every level* of the organization. Senior leaders may need better change leadership skills. Mid-level managers might need stronger project management tools. Frontline teams may need to learn new systems or workflows.

And most critically, it means giving people room to grow—without punishing them for learning curves.

## Capability Isn't Just Technical—It's Cultural

The best teams don't just have technical skills. They have *emotional readiness*. They can adapt, collaborate, and recover when plans shift. That's where the earlier investment in trust pays dividends—because people who trust their environment are more likely to stretch themselves in it.

And when people feel safe to learn, they grow. And when they grow, so does your capacity to execute.

**Ask Yourself:**
- What are the must-have capabilities to deliver this strategy?
- Where are the gaps—in skill, structure, or leadership?
- What's my plan to build or acquire what's missing?

The best strategies succeed not because they are easy, but because the team is equipped to do the hard things well.

Next, we'll explore how to ensure the *right* people are in the *right* roles—so you're not just developing talent, but deploying it wisely.

**Getting the Right People in the Right Seats**

Jim Collins famously said, "First who, then what."

You can have a brilliant strategy, a clear mission, and a deeply inspired purpose—but if the wrong people are in the key roles, or the right people are in the *wrong* roles, execution will suffer. Period.

The best leaders understand this early. They prioritize *who* before *how*. They don't build strategies and then scramble to find people to deliver them. They start by surrounding themselves with people who are not only capable—but *committed*, adaptable, and aligned with the mission.

## More Than Talent: It's About Fit

Getting the right people in the right seats doesn't just mean hiring high performers. It means putting people where their strengths *match the demands* of the role. It means understanding what energizes them, where they create the most value, and how they respond under pressure.

Because even top talent underperforms in the wrong environment. Misalignment creates friction. Friction creates frustration. Frustration kills momentum.

On the other hand, when people are in roles that tap into their strengths and values, something powerful happens: energy rises. Execution accelerates. Culture improves.

## A Leader's Job: Evaluate and Adjust

The best leaders constantly assess whether the current team is positioned to win:

- Do we have the right people *on* the team?
- Are they in roles that match their capabilities and aspirations?
- Are we being honest—with them and with ourselves—about what needs to change?

Sometimes that means coaching. Sometimes it means reassigning. And sometimes, it means making hard decisions to remove people who aren't a fit. Not out of punishment, but out of responsibility—to the mission, to the rest of the team, and to the person who may be better suited elsewhere.

**Don't Confuse Loyalty with Alignment**

One of the most difficult leadership traps is keeping someone in a role they've outgrown—or never fit—out of loyalty. But loyalty without alignment slows everyone down. You can care about someone and still know they're not in the right seat. Great leaders do both.

Getting the right people in the right seats isn't a one-time event. It's a continuous discipline. But when done well, it becomes one of the most powerful accelerators of execution.

In the next section, we'll tie it all together—by exploring how **influence, communication, and culture** amplify relationships and drive lasting change.

**Influence, Communication, and Culture**

Once you have trust, alignment, and the right people in the right seats, one question remains:

**Can you sustain it?**

That's where culture comes in.

Culture is the invisible force that shapes how things really get done. It lives in the space between policies and behavior. It determines whether people speak up or stay silent, collaborate or compete, commit or comply.

And here's the truth: **culture is shaped by communication and reinforced through influence.**

### Strategy Is Communicated in Moments, Not Memos

Leaders often overestimate how much their teams understand the strategy—and underestimate how often it needs to be repeated.

You can't expect alignment after one presentation. People don't just absorb information—they absorb *tone*, *trust*, and *consistency*. That means strategy must be communicated often, clearly, and through multiple channels—from the boardroom to the breakroom.

More importantly, it must be *lived*. Teams watch what leaders reward, what they tolerate, and what they model. That's how strategy becomes culture. When leaders communicate with clarity, act with integrity, and stay consistent under pressure, teams follow—not out of obligation, but belief.

### Influence Is Leadership Without a Title

Some of the most effective strategic leaders don't have CEO or VP in their titles. They influence by how they show up, how they build relationships, how they communicate vision, and how they move others toward shared outcomes.

If your team sees you listening, learning, adapting—they'll trust you. If they see you pushing through difficult conversations without flinching—they'll follow. If they see you putting mission over ego, they'll do the same.

That's how culture scales: one conversation, one decision, one leader at a time.

### Culture Doesn't Support Strategy—It *Is* Strategy

At the end of the day, the culture you build will either amplify your strategy or erode it. You can't bolt culture on after the plan is made. You have to build it into how the work gets done—from how meetings are run, to how feedback is given, to how recognition is earned.

Strategy fails when people don't feel heard. It thrives when they feel seen, valued, and trusted.

### Relationships Drive Results

Strong strategy is not just about smart plans—it's about strong people, aligned around a common mission, supported by trust, and enabled to thrive.

If you want to execute a bold strategy, start by investing in relationships. Because nothing scales faster—or fails faster—than the culture you build through people.

Chapter 3 Summary

- **Strategy depends on people.** Even the best plans fail without teams that are engaged, aligned, and committed.

- **Trust is the foundation.** It creates safety, accelerates decision-making, and sustains momentum in high-pressure environments. Without it, fear and misalignment stall progress.

- **Leadership is influence.** Strong relationships are built through consistency, honesty, listening, and vulnerability—not just authority.

- **Alignment drives execution.** Mission and purpose must be clearly communicated, understood, and owned at every level—not just written on a wall.

- **Capability is critical.** Alignment without skills, tools, and resources is just intention. Leaders must build and equip teams to deliver.

- **Right people, right seats.** Talent only thrives when roles fit strengths and values. Misalignment creates friction; alignment unlocks energy and execution.

- **Culture is strategy.** Strategy comes alive through daily communication, behaviors, and reinforcement. What leaders model and reward becomes culture.

- **Relationships multiply results.** When people trust each other, align around purpose, and feel equipped to succeed, strategy transforms from plan to performance.

# Chapter 4

# Ownership

## Create a Culture of Accountability

*"For the strength of the pack is the wolf, and the strength of the wolf is the pack."*
— *Rudyard Kipling*

There's a certain kind of energy you don't forget. You feel it in a high-performing team—focused, fast, and fully committed. Sparks fly—sometimes literally. People take initiative. They act like owners, not employees. They don't wait for instructions; they move.

That kind of energy doesn't happen by accident. It's the result of **ownership**.

I've seen firsthand how ownership can transform a business from the inside out. One of the clearest examples came when my partner and I founded **Wolfpack Chassis**—a startup we launched in 2012 with more grit than capital.

We named the company after Kipling's Law of the Jungle because we believed in what it stood for: *"The strength of the pack is the wolf, and the strength of the wolf is the pack."* We knew that if we were going to succeed, it wouldn't be because of a flashy product feature or market shortcut. It would be because we built a team that treated the mission as their own.

In the beginning, we had no real orders, no market reputation, and no room for passengers. I still remember yelling across the plant to my partner, "Hey Steve—know anyone who wants to buy some chassis?" He laughed and shouted back, "No, but I hope you do!"

It was part joke, part challenge. We had just opened our doors. The team was getting paid hourly with the promise of production bonuses—bonuses that hadn't materialized much yet. But they showed up. They believed in what we were building. More importantly, they took responsibility for making it happen.

They didn't just assemble chassis. They delivered exceptional results in quality, cost, and delivery. And as orders began to roll in, their ownership deepened. By year two, we were running a second shift, exceeding our business plan, and growing at 50% year over year.

**That's the power of ownership.**

Ownership turns a strategy from *something leaders tell people to do* into *something teams take personally*. It creates a culture where accountability isn't enforced—it's embraced.

In this chapter, we'll outline what it takes to build a true culture of ownership—from the front lines to the executive suite. You'll learn:

- Why clarity and alignment are prerequisites for accountability
- How to shift from compliance to commitment
- What behaviors and systems reinforce ownership at scale
- And how to deal with blame, excuses, and underperformance in a way that strengthens culture instead of weakening it

Because in the end, execution doesn't come from control. It comes from belief. And belief creates ownership. And ownership is another foundational part of strategy because it delivers results.

### Accountability Starts with Clarity

You can't hold people accountable for what they don't understand.

Before you can expect ownership, you must first create clarity—about *what* needs to be achieved, *why* it matters, and *who* is responsible. When expectations are vague, even talented, motivated teams will struggle. Confusion breeds frustration, and frustration kills momentum.

*"Ownership turns a strategy from something leaders tell people to do into something teams take personally."*

In a culture of real accountability, there's no ambiguity. People know exactly what success looks like, and they know whether or not they're hitting the mark.

**Clarity Drives Ownership**

Accountability isn't about micromanagement or metrics overload. It's about making commitments visible and measurable. Clarity answers questions like:

- What are the specific goals we're trying to achieve?
- Who is responsible for each one?
- How will we know when it's working—or when it's not?

Great leaders don't just set expectations—they *confirm understanding*. They don't assume alignment—they check for it. They create the conditions for ownership by removing uncertainty and defining outcomes clearly.

**What Gets Measured Gets Owned**

When metrics are clear and tied to a larger purpose, they stop feeling like surveillance and start feeling like direction. People want to know where they stand. They want to know their work has meaning. And the strongest teams don't shy away from numbers—they seek them out.

At Wolfpack Chassis, we kept our focus sharp: safety, quality, delivery, and cost. Every team member could see the connection between their efforts and the bigger picture. There was no guessing. Because expectations were visible and consistent, people stepped up without needing pressure.

That's the real value of clarity—it makes accountability not just possible, but natural.

**Ask Yourself:**

- Have I clearly defined what success looks like for every member of my team?

- Does each person understand how their role contributes to our broader mission?
- Are we measuring the right things—and are we reviewing results openly and regularly?

Up next, we'll look at what it takes to move from compliance to commitment. Because ownership isn't about completing tasks. It's about showing up like it matters.

**From Compliance to Commitment**

Compliance gets you effort. Commitment gets you results.

In a culture of compliance, people do what they're told. They show up, check the boxes, and avoid mistakes. It's not bad—but it's not greatness. Compliance is about obligation.

Commitment, on the other hand, is ownership in motion. It's when people care enough to go beyond the job description. They take initiative. They anticipate problems. They make decisions that move the mission forward—whether or not someone's watching.

The difference is night and day.

**You Can't Mandate Commitment**

Some of the best work happens when no one's watching. Not because someone was told to do it, but because they chose to care.

That's the difference between compliance and commitment. Compliance can be managed with rules and checklists. Commitment takes something deeper. It grows when people feel connected to the purpose behind their work, when they're trusted to think for themselves, and when their input actually shapes outcomes.

People rise when they feel valued. When they see that what they do matters, not just to their manager, but to the mission as a whole. That belief creates buy-in. And with buy-in comes momentum.

If your team believes in the goal, in each other, and in their role within it, they'll do more than show up; they'll take ownership. You won't have to push. They'll already be in motion.

### From Control to Empowerment

The shift from compliance to commitment also requires a shift in leadership. You move from controlling every detail to *empowering people with clear outcomes and trusting them to deliver.*

At Wolfpack Chassis, we didn't micromanage. We defined what great looked like and gave people room to own it. We held the bar high, but we gave them the tools, autonomy, and support to meet it. That ownership led to extraordinary commitment—from the shop floor to the leadership team.

It wasn't about enforcing rules. It was about reinforcing belief.

### Ask Yourself:

- Are we managing to rules or leading to outcomes?
- Do our systems reward initiative—or just obedience?
- Are we building a culture where people feel trusted and empowered?

In the next section, we'll explore the structures and systems that **reinforce ownership at scale**—so that it's not just one leader driving results, but a culture that multiplies it.

**Reinforcing Ownership at Scale**

Ownership isn't just a leadership mindset—it must become an organizational habit.

You might have a few team members who naturally take ownership. But if you want sustained, repeatable performance, you need **systems that support it.** Without structure, ownership erodes over time. Good intentions give way to busy schedules. Strategic focus gives way to firefighting. And eventually, accountability becomes optional.

To make ownership stick, you need **reinforcing mechanisms**—tools, rhythms, and cultural signals that turn it from a value into a behavior.

**1. Establish a Cadence of Accountability**

Regular performance check-ins, team huddles, and KPI reviews aren't just administrative rituals—they're how you keep ownership visible. A well-run weekly meeting can do more to reinforce accountability than a dozen emails or policy memos.

Make it a habit to review:

- Key objectives
- Progress and obstacles
- Ownership by name (who is responsible for what)
- Lessons learned

When everyone knows the score, and everyone sees where they fit into it, accountability becomes a shared expectation—not a surprise.

**2. Make Success—and Gaps—Visible**

What gets celebrated gets repeated. What gets ignored gets forgotten.

People lean into what they feel seen for. When progress is acknowledged, it motivates more of it. When silence follows effort, momentum fades.

If you're trying to build ownership, start by recognizing it out loud. Celebrate small wins. Call out the moments when someone took initiative or stepped up without being asked. These signals matter—they show the team what's valued.

But visibility isn't just about praise. Gaps need attention too. That doesn't mean pointing fingers—it means naming what's not working with honesty and respect. Ownership doesn't require perfection; it requires shared responsibility.

When leaders are transparent, it invites the same from the team. That openness builds trust. And trust is what turns effort into engagement, and engagement into results.

### 3. Align Incentives with Impact

People need to see that ownership is not only expected—it's rewarded. That doesn't always mean money. Recognition, development opportunities, and autonomy can be just as powerful. The key is to align what you reward with the behaviors that drive results.

At Wolfpack Chassis, we tied production bonuses not just to output, but to quality and team collaboration. The message was clear: your individual performance matters—but so does your impact on the whole. That alignment fueled a culture where people watched out for each other and pushed together toward common goals.

**Ask Yourself:**

- Do we have a rhythm that keeps accountability front and center?
- Are we consistently recognizing and reinforcing ownership behaviors?
- Do our incentives support the kind of culture we want to build?

Ownership at scale isn't about heroic individuals. It's about consistent systems and a culture that says: *we don't wait for someone else to lead—we own it together.*

In the final section of this chapter, we'll look at how to confront **blame, excuses, and underperformance**—not with fear, but with a mindset that strengthens accountability and builds a more resilient team.

**Dealing with Blame, Excuses, and Underperformance**

Every team faces moments when things fall short. A deadline is missed. A deliverable fails to meet the mark. A promise goes unfulfilled. These are not just operational issues but cultural tests.

What happens in those moments reveals what your organization truly values. Do people step forward, or step back? Do they take responsibility, or shift it elsewhere? The answer depends on the culture you've built around accountability.

In a healthy culture of ownership, underperformance isn't ignored—and it isn't punished. It's addressed with honesty and a shared desire to improve. The goal isn't to find fault, but to find footing. Progress only happens when people feel safe enough to be honest and strong enough to face the truth.

But when blame becomes the default, people protect themselves instead of the mission. When excuses go unchecked, standards quietly drop. And when underperformance is tolerated, others take note—and expectations start to drift.

Accountability, at its best, is about alignment. It's the collective agreement that we hold each other—not just to tasks, but to a level of care, focus, and integrity that reflects our purpose.

What you choose to correct and what you choose to let slide speaks volumes. Culture isn't built in the wins alone—it's shaped in how you handle what didn't go right, and who you invite into the process of making it better.

**Set the Tone: No Blame, No Excuses**

Great leaders model accountability. They own their decisions, admit when they're wrong, and expect the same from others. That tone sets the standard. It tells the team: *We don't hide from problems—we make them visible and solve them together.*

When someone drops the ball, start with curiosity, not criticism:

- What happened?
- What did we learn?
- What will we do differently next time?

That doesn't mean lowering the bar. It means raising the standard for how you deal with failure. The goal isn't to avoid mistakes—it's to become the kind of team that learns fast and adapts forward.

### Call It Early and Address It Directly

One of the most dangerous things a leader can do is delay a tough conversation. When you don't address underperformance, you're signaling that the culture doesn't mean what it says.

Accountability conversations don't have to be harsh—but they do have to be honest. Be clear. Be specific. Show care, but don't sugarcoat. The best team members will appreciate the clarity, and the ones who don't probably weren't fully committed to begin with.

### Accountability Is a Two-Way Street

If you want your team to take ownership, you have to own your role too. Did they have the resources? The support? The clarity? The coaching? Leaders who ask those questions create a culture of shared accountability, not one-sided judgment.

And that's the kind of culture where ownership thrives.

### Ask Yourself:

- Are we confronting underperformance with clarity and care—or avoiding it?
- Do we treat mistakes as learning opportunities—or as failures to be punished?
- Are we modeling the kind of accountability we want to see?

**The Discipline of Ownership**

Ownership isn't just about individual behavior. It's a culture. A system. A set of shared expectations that say: *We are responsible for the results we create—together.*

It starts with clarity. It grows through commitment. It's reinforced by structure. And it's sustained by a leader's willingness to face the hard things head-on.

Because when people take ownership, everything changes. Execution accelerates. Teams gel. Results compound.

And strategy stops being a presentation—and becomes a way of life.

When ownership is embedded in the culture, strategy stops being something that belongs to the top and starts being something everyone owns. People no longer just execute tasks; they take accountability for outcomes.

However, ownership alone isn't enough.

For an organization to win with strategy, every team, function, and individual must understand how their work connects to the bigger picture. In the next chapter, we'll explore how to cascade and align strategy across all segments of the organization—so that everyone is not only accountable, but also strategically connected to the mission.

## Chapter 4 Summary

- **Ownership creates energy.** Teams move faster, think sharper, and take initiative when they feel responsible for outcomes—not just tasks.

- **Clarity is the foundation.** People can't own what they don't understand. Clear goals, roles, and measures remove ambiguity and make accountability natural.

- **Metrics matter.** What gets measured gets owned. Visible results tied to purpose give meaning to work and motivate performance.

- **Commitment beats compliance.** Compliance gets effort; commitment drives results. Ownership grows when people believe in the mission and are trusted to deliver.

- **Leadership shifts from control to empowerment.** Great leaders set outcomes, provide tools, and create space for initiative—instead of managing every detail.

- **Systems sustain ownership.** Cadences of accountability, visible progress, and aligned incentives embed ownership into culture and make it scalable.

- **Accountability strengthens culture.** Addressing blame, excuses, and underperformance directly—but with care—reinforces trust, resilience, and high standards.

- **Ownership is collective.** True strategy comes alive when everyone—from the front line to the executive suite—embraces responsibility for results.

## Chapter 5

## Strategy

Choose the Right How

*"The essence of strategy is choosing what not to do."*
— Michael Porter

If focus defines what you're aiming for, and relationships and ownership align people around that aim, then strategy answers the next critical question:

**How are we going to win?**

Strategy connects vision to execution. It's what turns ambition into movement and ideas into direction. But it's not just about drafting a plan—it's about making a series of deliberate, informed choices. The strongest strategies are rooted in reality, shaped by insight, and guided by discipline. They don't appear by accident. They're built.

At its core, strategy is the method by which individuals and organizations pursue their goals. And because most teams are working toward more than one objective, they often need more than one strategy in play. That's why success requires clarity about what matters most and how each piece of the mission will be achieved.

Strategy also operates on different levels. At the highest level, the focus level, it defines your mission, purpose, vision, and strategic objectives. These provide direction for the entire organization. But those top-level objectives need more than just alignment; they need traction. And that comes from supporting strategies: focused plans that break big goals into meaningful, executable steps.

When built with intention, this layered approach helps organizations stay clear and connected while moving in many directions at once. Strategy becomes the thread that runs through every level, tying aspiration to daily action. It ensures that people at every layer of the business, from executives to front-line teams, know where the organization is headed, what success looks like, and how they're helping make it happen.

The strategic alignment cascade below offers a real-world example of how these layers come together.

Chapter 7 builds on this by introducing the Strategic Planning Canvas, a practical tool to help you bring that alignment to life across your entire organization.

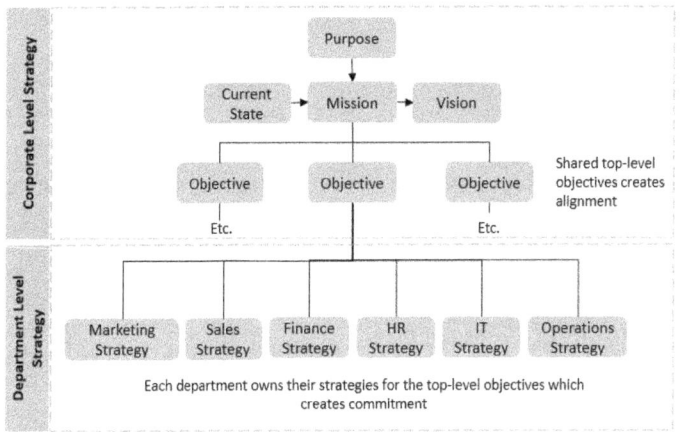

## Strategic Alignment Cascade

### Strategy Begins with Focus

Strategy doesn't begin with ideas on a whiteboard. It begins with clarity.

Before any plan can take shape, you need to be sure of what matters most. Focus is that foundation. It anchors your purpose, aligns your mission and vision, defines your current reality, and sets the objectives that move everything forward. These objectives are not just tasks to complete; they're the true north that guide your direction.

Every decision, every initiative, every investment should pass through a single, honest filter:

### Does this move us closer to our objectives?

If not, it's a distraction. If it does, it deserves attention.

That's what strategic discipline looks like. It's not just about choosing what to pursue—it's about learning to let go of what doesn't serve the bigger goal. When focus leads, strategy becomes sharper, execution becomes easier, and progress becomes measurable.

### Strategy Is the "How" Behind the "What"

Think of it this way: your **objectives define what success looks like.** Your **strategy defines how you'll get there.** The two must be linked. If your strategy isn't clearly aligned to your objectives, you're either chasing the wrong priorities—or you don't have a real strategy at all.

This is why effective leaders start by asking:

- What are we trying to accomplish?
- What are the few critical paths that will get us there?
- What trade-offs must we make to stay aligned?

Strategy isn't about exploring every idea—it's about *committing to the right few*, with relentless discipline.

### Let Your Objectives Be the Filter

When you're faced with competing opportunities, shiny new ideas, or requests from every corner of the business, come back to this question:

**Does this help us achieve the objectives of our mission and, ultimately, realize our vision?**

If the answer is no, be willing to walk away. Strategic clarity is just as much about subtraction as it is about direction. The most successful organizations—and individuals—aren't defined by how much they do, but by how much of what they do *actually matters*.

### Designing Strategic Initiatives That Deliver

Once you've defined your objectives and chosen your strategic priorities, the next step is translating those choices into action. That means designing **strategic initiatives**—the focused programs and projects that will move the needle.

This is where strategy becomes visible. It's where teams rally, resources get mobilized, and progress is measured. But here's the key: **not all initiatives are strategic.** Many are just activities. And activity without alignment is the fastest path to burnout without results.

So the question becomes:

**Are we building initiatives that directly support our objectives?**

If the answer isn't a confident yes, you're not designing strategy—you're just staying busy.

### Start with a Strategy Map

One of the most effective tools for aligning initiatives with objectives is a simple **strategy map**—a one-page visual that shows:

- Your core focus areas (linked to mission and vision)
- Your objectives (what must be achieved)
- Your strategic initiatives (how you'll get there)

This forces clarity. It eliminates ambiguity. And it makes it much easier to say *no* to things that don't matter.

**From Idea to Initiative**

To turn an idea into a winning initiative, ask:
1. Which objective does this support?
2. What outcome will it produce—and how will we measure it?
3. What resources will it require (time, people, budget)?
4. What's the timeline, and who owns it?
5. What risks or obstacles need to be addressed?

If an initiative can't answer those questions, it's not ready for execution.

**The Discipline of Fewer, Bigger Bets**

One of the hallmarks of great strategy is **focus**—not just in vision, but in execution. That means choosing a few big bets, not dozens of disconnected activities.

Spreading resources thin across too many priorities dilutes impact. Concentrating resources on a focused set of strategic initiatives creates momentum, accelerates results, and builds confidence across the organization.

When people see real progress, they lean in. When they see chaos, they check out.

**Ask Yourself:**

- Are our strategic initiatives clearly aligned to our objectives?
- Do we have the resources and leadership in place to execute each one?
- Are we focusing on a few high-impact efforts—or trying to do everything?

In the next section, we'll shift from strategy to tactics—where day-to-day execution begins, and where plans either come to life or fall short.

## Chapter 5 Summary

- **Strategy answers the question: How will we win?** It connects vision to execution by turning ambition into deliberate, disciplined choices.

- **Focus comes first.** Strategy begins with clarity—anchoring mission, vision, and objectives so every initiative can be filtered through what matters most.

- **Objectives define the "what"; strategy defines the "how."** If the two aren't linked, you don't have a real strategy—you have activity without direction.

- **Strategic clarity requires trade-offs.** Saying yes to the right few priorities means having the discipline to say no to distractions.

- **Initiatives bring strategy to life.** True strategic initiatives are tightly aligned to objectives; activity without alignment is wasted effort.

- **Tools like strategy maps create alignment.** A simple, visual map links focus areas, objectives, and initiatives—making it easier to drive clarity and consistency.

- **The power of fewer, bigger bets.** Concentrating resources on a select set of high-impact initiatives accelerates progress, builds momentum, and strengthens confidence.

- **Discipline sustains execution.** When strategy is clear, focused, and reinforced with structured initiatives, it becomes the thread that ties aspiration to daily action.

Chapter 6

Tactics

Execute with Discipline

*"You do not rise to the level of your goals. You fall to the level of your systems."*
—James Clear

Strategy sets the direction. But **tactics create the movement.**

Even the best strategy will fail without disciplined, consistent action. Tactics are where the rubber meets the road—where ideas become work, and where focus, relationships, and ownership are tested daily.

The organizations that win aren't just the ones with great plans. They're the ones that **execute with precision and discipline**, week after week, month after month.

## Tactics Turn Strategy into Motion

If strategy is the "how," then tactics are the **what, when, and by whom**. They're the specific actions, routines, and systems that bring a strategic initiative to life.

Let's say your strategy includes "Expand into new customer segments."

The tactical layer might include:

- Launching a new marketing campaign
- Training the sales team on a revised value proposition
- Developing a localized product variation
- Setting a target for 25% revenue growth in a new vertical

These are **tactical actions**—clear, time-bound, and owned by specific individuals or teams. They move the strategy forward in real, measurable ways.

> *"The organizations that win aren't just the ones with great plans. They're the ones that execute with precision and discipline, week after week, month after month."*

## Execution Requires Rhythm and Rigor

Winning teams don't rely on willpower or good intentions. They rely on **systems and cadence**.

That might mean:

- Weekly action reviews
- Monthly progress dashboards
- Quarterly strategy checkpoints
- Defined accountability structures

Without a consistent operating rhythm, even the clearest strategy will fade into background noise. But when teams get into a healthy cadence—where goals are reviewed, blockers removed, and wins celebrated—execution becomes a habit.

### Focus on Leading Indicators

Most organizations wait too long to find out if execution is working. They track lagging metrics—like revenue, profit, or growth—but miss the **leading indicators** that signal progress.

Examples of leading indicators:

- Number of customer meetings scheduled
- Time-to-resolution on service tickets
- Milestone completion rates
- On-time project deliverables

By tracking these, you can adjust in real time—*before* the big results are won or lost. Chapter 2 of *The 4 Disciplines of Execution* (McChesney et al.) explores Discipline 2: **Act on the Lead Measures**, offering a clear and practical framework for identifying and selecting high-impact leading indicators.

### Anticipate Problems Before They Happen

One of the most overlooked aspects of execution is **proactive risk management.** Far too often, teams only deal with problems when they've already turned into fire drills. But the most disciplined organizations **anticipate issues early and respond with precision.**

That's not just good project hygiene—it's good leadership.

High-performing teams make risk management part of their daily execution rhythm. They don't wait for surprises. They build **systems that surface them early**—before they derail timelines, damage morale, or burn through budgets.

## Use Tools, Not Just Intuition

Risk management doesn't need to be complicated, but it must be intentional. Here are three proven tools that help teams stay on the front foot:

- **Risk Log:**
  A running list of potential risks—what could go wrong, what the impact would be, and what's being done about it. This makes risks visible, trackable, and owned.
- **Action Tracker:**
  A disciplined way to follow up on who's doing what by when—especially for decisions, deliverables, or risk mitigations. A great strategy fails when accountability is vague.
- **RAID Log (Risks, Assumptions, Issues, Dependencies):**
  A comprehensive tracker that captures not only risks and issues, but also the assumptions you're relying on and the dependencies that could slow things down.

The best teams **review these logs regularly**—weekly, biweekly, or monthly depending on project complexity. They use them to spark productive conversations, allocate resources, and remove blockers early.

## Create a Culture of Candor, Not Crisis

When risk management is treated as a checklist or an afterthought, it becomes a burden. But when it's built into the culture—when people are encouraged to surface risks early and without fear—it becomes a strength.

Execution doesn't mean avoiding problems. It means **having the courage to face them, and the systems to deal with them before they escalate.**

**Ask Yourself:**
- What's likely to get in our way?
- Who owns each risk—and what's the mitigation plan?
- Are we actively managing issues, or reacting to them too late?

**From 50% to 95%: Turning Execution into a Competitive Advantage**

At Zimmer Biomet, I had the opportunity to lead a global transformation of our program delivery organization. When I stepped into the role as Global Director of Program Management, the strategic project success rate hovered around 50%. Projects were regularly missing key milestones, and accountability was inconsistent. Everyone was working hard—but we weren't winning consistently.

So we set out to change that—not with slogans or quick fixes, but by building a disciplined, system-driven approach to execution.

We implemented a standardized project management lifecycle, grounded in agile principles but strengthened by structure. We focused relentlessly on leading indicators of success, tracking eight critical dimensions of project health:

- Overall progress
- Cost

- Schedule
- Scope
- Resources
- Risks
- Dependencies
- Business benefits

Each was evaluated weekly using a simple red-yellow-green system, visible in a portfolio-wide dashboard. If even one metric signaled trouble, the overall project status turned yellow or red—ensuring visibility, accountability, and most importantly, timely action.

But visibility alone doesn't drive results. What changed the game was our rhythm.

Any project flagged yellow or red was required to attend a weekly health check—not as a punitive exercise, but as a support mechanism. These sessions brought the right leaders to the table quickly, so we could understand the root issue, mobilize resources, and course-correct before problems escalated.

Over time, the culture shifted. Escalation wasn't seen as failure—it was seen as discipline. It was a sign that we were serious about execution. Teams became proactive. Status meetings became focused. Momentum accelerated.

**The result?**

We lifted our strategic project success rate from 50% to consistently over 95%. The team was nominated for Project Management Institute's PMO of the Year—a testament not just to what we built, but how we built it: with systems, with discipline, and with an unwavering commitment to deliver on what mattered most.

That's how execution transforms from a routine into a competitive weapon —when your ability to deliver strategic value better, faster, and more consistently than the competition becomes not just an edge, but a defining advantage.

**Eliminate the Noise**

Discipline in execution also means **saying no** to distractions. Tactics must be aligned with strategy—and strategy must be aligned with objectives. Anything that doesn't support that chain is noise. And noise is the enemy of execution.

Great leaders protect their teams from that noise. They create clarity, simplify priorities, and ensure the team stays locked in on what matters most.

**Ask Yourself:**

- Are our tactics clearly mapped to each strategic initiative?
- Do we have a system to track progress and adjust in real time?
- Are we focused—or just busy?

With discipline in tactics, alignment across strategy, and a foundation of focus, relationships, and ownership—you don't just create plans. You create results.

## Chapter 6 Summary

- **Tactics bring strategy to life.** They define the *what, when, and by whom*—the concrete actions that move big ideas forward.

- **Execution requires rhythm and rigor.** Weekly reviews, monthly dashboards, and quarterly checkpoints create a cadence where accountability and progress become habits.

- **Leading indicators matter.** Tracking early signals (like milestone completion or customer meetings) enables timely adjustments before big results are won or lost.

- **Anticipate risks proactively.** High-performing teams surface risks early and manage them with tools like risk logs, action trackers, and RAID logs.

- **Build a culture of candor, not crisis.** Encourage openness about obstacles—when risks are raised early, solutions come faster and trust deepens.

- **Systematic discipline drives results.** At Zimmer Biomet, moving to a structured, metrics-driven approach to execution raised project success rates from 50% to over 95%.

- **Focus by eliminating noise.** Tactics only matter if they align to strategy; distractions drain momentum and dilute results.

- **Execution becomes a competitive advantage.** The organizations that win aren't just those with the best strategies, but those that deliver with consistency, precision, and discipline.

## Chapter 7

## Bringing It All Together

### From Process to Action

*"Vision without action is a daydream. Action without vision is a nightmare."*
—*Japanese Proverb*

You've now seen how each piece of the FROST Strategy Pyramid fits together. From purpose to performance, from people to plans, this model is designed to close the gap between **strategy and execution**—and to do it in a way that honors both the emotional and logical sides of transformation.

Now it's time to bring it all together. But first, let's revisit the five elements, not as theory, but as a connected system for results:

- **Focus**: Clarity of purpose. Define your mission, your why, your vision of success, your current state, and the objectives that will turn vision into reality. Focus is where alignment begins.

- **Relationships:** Everything happens through people. Strategy succeeds when trust, communication, and shared commitment are strong. Influence is built on relationships—and relationships are built on respect.
- **Ownership:** Execution only happens when people take responsibility. It's not about titles; it's about commitment. Create a culture where accountability is expected, modeled, and reinforced.
- **Strategy:** The "how" that turns focus into movement. Choose the right priorities, say no to the wrong ones, and align every initiative with your objectives. Strategy is about making disciplined, intentional choices.
- **Tactics:** Turn strategy into consistent action. Build systems, create cadence, track the right metrics, and execute with discipline. Tactics are where progress becomes performance.

These five elements don't work in isolation—they work in harmony. Each reinforces the others. Together, they form a complete approach to strategic success.

### From Framework to Facilitation: The Strategic Planning Canvas

To make this system truly actionable, I developed a one-page tool called the **FROST Strategic Planning Canvas**—a practical, visual way to apply the FROST Strategy Pyramid to any strategic challenge.

Inspired by the simplicity of the Business Model Canvas, the Strategic Planning Canvas is designed to:

## Strategic Planning Canvas™
*Strategy on a Page*

### ❶ FOCUS

**Purpose**
Why does it matter? What is the higher cause that we are passionate about?

**Mission**
What are we doing?

**Vision**
Where are we going? What does success look like?

**Current State**
Where are we today? What is our starting point?

**Objectives**
What are the measurable goals we need to achieve to complete our mission?

### ❷ RELATIONSHIPS
Who is critical to success? How will we build trust and shared commitment?

### ❹ STRATEGIES
How will we achieve the objectives? What focused initiatives will move us forward?

### ❸ OWNERSHIP
Who is responsible and accountable for what? Are the owners aligned and committed?

### ❺ TACTICS
What detailed steps are needed to deliver the strategies? What are the key milestones, timelines and metrics?

© 2025 Frostline Strategy Group LLC

- Clarify your mission, vision, and objectives
- Identify and prioritize strategic initiatives
- Map ownership and team alignment
- Track tactical execution and key metrics
- Facilitate strategic planning and ongoing performance reviews

Whether you're working with a leadership team, guiding a department, running a nonprofit, or pursuing personal goals, the Strategic Planning Canvas helps keep everyone aligned on what matters most—and how you're going to achieve it.

The Strategic Planning Canvas can also be used at all levels of the organization to drive alignment and commitment as shown in the business example below.

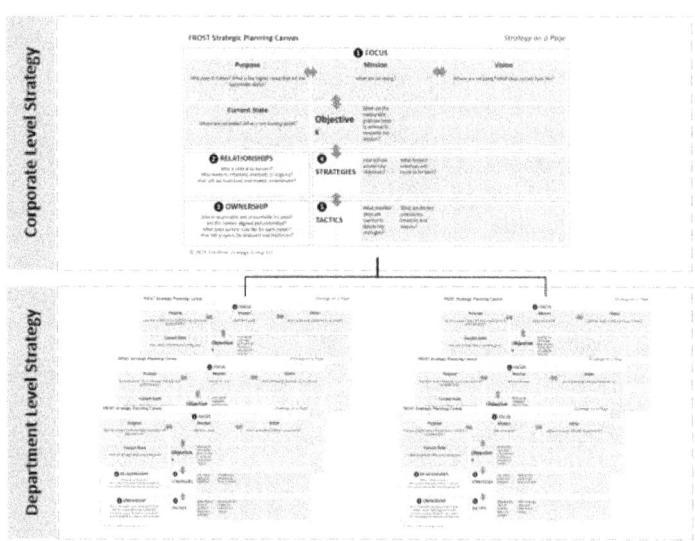

Cascading the Strategic Planning Canvas to Drive Alignment and Commitment

It's not just a planning tool. It's a **realization tool**—built to drive commitment, action, and results.

## Why This Matters

Too often, strategy becomes a document that sits on a shelf. The plan is thoughtful. The intent is real. But the execution falls apart because people were never fully aligned—or fully committed.

The FROST Strategy Pyramid and Strategic Planning Canvas are built to change that.

They bring clarity where there's confusion. Connection where there's fragmentation. And momentum where things feel stuck.

This is a framework that works in boardrooms, classrooms, operating rooms, and living rooms. Because at its core, it's not just about organizations—it's about **people doing important work with focus, discipline, and purpose.**

> *"Whether you're working with a leadership team, guiding a department, running a nonprofit, or pursuing personal goals, the Strategic Planning Canvas helps keep everyone aligned on what matters most—and how you're going to achieve it."*

## What's Next

In the chapters that follow, we'll explore real-world examples of how this framework has been used across industries and settings—from startups to Fortune 500s, from community initiatives to personal transformations.

The appendix also provides step-by-step guidance for facilitating a planning session and completing the Strategic

Planning Canvas, serving as your hands-on toolkit to bring the Strategic Planning Canvas to life.

Because strategy isn't just for high-stakes corporate initiatives. It's for *anything worth doing well.*

Let's see what that looks like in practice.

## Chapter 7 Summary

- **The FROST Strategy Pyramid works as a system.** Focus, Relationships, Ownership, Strategy, and Tactics reinforce one another, creating a complete framework for turning vision into results.

- **Focus sets the foundation.** Define purpose, mission, vision, current state, and objectives to create alignment and clarity.

- **Relationships drive influence.** Trust, respect, and shared commitment enable strategy to succeed through people.

- **Ownership fuels execution.** Accountability isn't about titles—it's about commitment at every level.

- **Strategy provides direction.** Make intentional choices, prioritize wisely, and align every initiative with objectives.

- **Tactics create momentum.** Systems, cadence, and disciplined action transform plans into measurable performance.

- **The Strategic Planning Canvas makes it actionable.** A simple, one-page tool to:
    - Clarify mission, vision, and objectives
    - Prioritize initiatives
    - Map ownership and alignment
    - Track execution and metrics
    - Facilitate ongoing reviews

- **From planning to realization.** The Canvas turns ideas into action, ensuring strategy doesn't gather dust but drives alignment, commitment, and results.

- **Why it matters.** Strategy often fails not from poor ideas, but from lack of alignment and execution. The FROST model and Canvas bring clarity, connection, and momentum.

- **Applicable everywhere.** Boardrooms, classrooms, nonprofits, healthcare, or personal goals—the framework helps people achieve what matters most.

## Chapter 8

## Strategy Realization

Make Winning the Only Option

*"The best way to predict the future is to create it."*
—Peter Drucker

I've always believed that just as there are physical laws—like gravity—that govern the universe, there are equally powerful **laws of winning** that govern achievement. They may be harder to see, but they are no less real. Among them, one stands above the rest: **belief**.

Back in Chapter 1, I said you can accomplish anything with the right strategy. Looking back, I should have said: you can accomplish anything with the right **attitude** *and* the right **strategy**.

If you believe in something strongly enough—if your vision is clear, your purpose is compelling, and your team is aligned—you will find a way to make it happen. Belief is what turns strategy from a plan into a force. And when belief is combined with discipline, alignment, and structure, **winning becomes not just possible—but inevitable.**

This chapter is about realizing that win. It's about pulling all the pieces of strategy together and applying them in a way that **makes winning the only option.**

### From Structure to Momentum

If you've followed the strategy process outlined in this book—starting with Focus, building Relationships, creating Ownership, selecting Strategy, and executing through Tactics—you now have all the ingredients for success.

As a certified Project Management Professional (PMP), one of the tools I've found most effective in bringing structure to execution is the **Work Breakdown Structure (WBS).** In project management, the WBS is a product-oriented "family tree" that breaks down a complex initiative into smaller, actionable components. Each level gets more detailed, more concrete, and more manageable.

*"All successful people have agreed in being causationists".*

*Ralph Waldo Emerson*

I've applied this same logic to strategy realization.

- At the top sits your **Mission**—the core of what you're trying to accomplish.
- Beneath that are the **Objectives**—your measurable targets.
- Under those lie your **Strategies**—the big, bold initiatives to reach the objectives.

- And at the foundation are your **Tactics**—the day-to-day actions that make it all move.

Ralph Waldo Emerson said "All successful people have agreed in being causationists". This cascading structure creates **cause-and-effect clarity**. If you've done the work upfront—built a focused mission, cultivated trust through relationships, created a culture of ownership, chosen the right strategic priorities—then the rest becomes a logical and executable process to create the effects you desire. And the system works like this:

If you execute the **tactics**, then you will deliver the **strategies**. If you deliver the **strategies**, then you will achieve the **objectives**. If you achieve the **objectives**, then you will fulfill the **mission**. And if you fulfill the **mission**, then you will realize your **purpose and vision**.

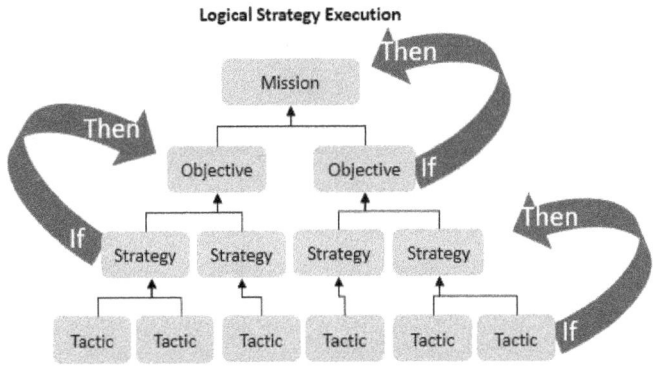

Strategy Execution WBS

This is more than a framework. It's a **chain of causation**—and when it's aligned, it creates unstoppable momentum.

**Strategy Realization in Action**

In the sections that follow, we'll walk through real-world examples of this process in motion:

- How a business strategy was brought to life through disciplined execution and team alignment
- How a complex program strategy succeeded despite cross-functional challenges
- How the same principles were applied to achieve a personal goal— and can you help you with your personal goals or a personal transformation

In every case, success didn't happen by accident. It was the result of belief, clarity, alignment, and disciplined execution.

When you bring those elements together—when you combine purpose with process, people with ownership, and ideas with action—**you make winning the only option.**

**Real-World Strategy Realization: Wolfpack Chassis - Building a Business from the Ground Up**

When my partner and I launched **Wolfpack Chassis**, we weren't just founding a company—we were putting strategy into motion from day one. We had no customers, no brand recognition, and no safety net. What we did have was a clear mission, a powerful sense of purpose, and an unshakable belief in the power of execution.

The name *Wolfpack* came from Rudyard Kipling's *Law of the Jungle*:

"For the strength of the pack is the wolf, and the strength of the wolf is the pack."

That wasn't just a slogan—it was a mindset. We believed that if we could build a tightly aligned, deeply committed team, we could win in a tough, price-sensitive, and highly competitive industry. And we did.

**FOCUS: Strategy Begins with Clarity**

From the start, we defined our focus with the same rigor as a Fortune 500 strategic plan—because when you're starting from scratch, there's no room for confusion.

- **Purpose:**
  To create shared success through performance—building great products, strong relationships, and opportunities for growth.
- **Mission:**
  To design and deliver world-class chassis systems with best-in-class quality, cost, and delivery—and earn customer loyalty through consistent performance.
- **Vision:**
  To become the most trusted chassis supplier in our category and a top-tier employer known for culture, craftsmanship, and customer excellence.
- **Current State:**
  We had no orders, no brand, and only a handful of employees—all relying on sweat equity, belief, and hustle.
- **Objectives:**
  1. Achieve operational break-even within 12 months.
  2. Exceed industry standards for quality and on-time delivery.
  3. Launch a second production shift within two years.

4. Build a culture of ownership, pride, and performance.

## RELATIONSHIPS: Strength Through Alignment

Relationships were at the core of everything. We couldn't afford misalignment or disengagement—every person had to be all-in.

- We hired people who believed in the mission and were willing to take personal ownership.
- We worked closely with suppliers and early customers to build credibility and trust.
- And we fostered peer-to-peer accountability across the team, not just top-down directives.

Every person mattered. In a small startup, culture is either your greatest multiplier—or your Achilles heel. We made culture our edge.

## OWNERSHIP: A Culture of Accountability

At Wolfpack, **ownership wasn't optional**—it was the expectation.

- We created incentive-based compensation tied directly to team performance.
- We held daily production huddles where frontline workers could raise issues and solve problems.
- Everyone had visibility into performance metrics—and a stake in improving them.

When people feel they own the outcome, they show up differently. They solve problems, not just identify them. They go the extra mile—because it's *their* mile.

## STRATEGY: A Two-Pronged Approach

We focused on two strategic pillars:

1. **People First:**
   Hire for mindset, train for skill. Build a team of believers, not just employees.
2. **Operational Excellence:**
   Deliver more value—faster, leaner, and more reliably—than the competition. Let performance speak louder than marketing.

We couldn't outspend our competitors on sales or advertising. But we could **out-execute** them. That was our edge.

## TACTICS: Turning Strategy into Reality

Execution happened through a disciplined, hands-on approach:

- We implemented **visual management systems**: production boards, floor metrics, and issue trackers.
- We held **cross-functional problem-solving sessions** to continuously improve operations.
- We scaled **intelligently**, doubling our systems along with our volume—not after the fact.

This wasn't just about building chassis. It was about building capability. As orders picked up, so did performance—because the systems were ready.

**RESULT: Strategy Realized Through Cause and Effect**

By the end of our second year, we had:

- Launched a second production shift
- Achieved a **compound annual growth rate (CAGR) of over 50%**
- Exceeded our profitability targets
- Built a culture where **pride and performance were inseparable**

This wasn't luck or timing. It was **strategy, executed through focus and ownership.**

We didn't just hope for results. We engineered them. Every tactic supported a strategy, every strategy drove an objective, every objective moved us closer to our mission—and our mission brought our purpose to life.

That's the power of cause-and-effect execution.

That's what **strategy realization** looks like when it's done right.

**Real-World Strategy Realization Example: Zimmer Biomet Sales Conversion Program**

At Zimmer Biomet, we had a bold aspiration: **to improve more patient lives every year.** But we faced a challenge common to many market leaders—the reconstructive hip and knee markets were mature, saturated, and flat. In a stagnant market, impact doesn't come from expansion—it comes from **winning share.**

We used the **FROST framework** to chart a course forward and execute with precision.

**FOCUS: Clarity That Drives Action**

- **Purpose:** Increase the number of patient lives positively impacted each year.
- **Mission:** Grow faster than the market.
- **Vision:** Become the world's leading musculoskeletal company by improving patient quality of life globally.
- **Current State:** The hip and knee markets were no longer growing. So the only way to reach more patients was to **convert competitive surgeons** to Zimmer Biomet solutions.
- **Objectives:**
    1. Convert at least **five major competitive surgeons.**
    2. Achieve revenue growth **10% above market.**

**RELATIONSHIPS: Aligning the Right Team**

Execution depended on more than just tactics—it required a cross-functional coalition of committed partners:

- **The Leadership Team** was aligned and fully supportive of the initiative.
- **Marketing** developed messaging that clearly differentiated Zimmer Biomet products.
- **IT** engineered the digital tools needed to scale communication and sales effectiveness.
- **Sales and Distribution** carried the message into the field, targeting and converting high-potential surgeons.
- And critically, **the surgeons themselves**—our customers—had to be influenced through credibility, consistency, and compelling value.

**OWNERSHIP:** Driving Accountability Across the Organization

From senior leadership to frontline sales reps, **everyone owned the outcome.** There were no excuses—just shared commitment. The culture was clear: **if we believe in the mission, we each have a role to play in achieving it.**

**STRATEGY: Choose the Right "How"**

Two key strategies formed the backbone of our effort:

1. **Develop targeted marketing programs** for competitive surgeons, clearly communicating the clinical and operational benefits of Zimmer Biomet solutions.
2. **Equip our sales and distribution teams with digital tools** to sharpen their ability to convert surgeons and address objections in real time.

**TACTICS: Bringing the Strategy to Life**

We translated our strategies into two critical, high-impact tactics:

- **Tactic 1: Zimmer Biomet Sales Intelligence (ZSI) App**
  We built a dynamic iPad-based tool that gave reps a real-time, point-of-care advantage. The ZSI app allowed sales professionals to instantly compare Zimmer Biomet products to competitor offerings—and more importantly, to deliver compelling, objective responses to surgeon objections, grounded in data and performance.
- **Tactic 2: National Launch at Sales Meeting**
  We launched ZSI at the national sales meeting, providing every sales rep with a new iPad preloaded

with the app. The launch was a showcase of belief and alignment: Zimmer Biomet senior leaders joined forces with Apple executives to present the initiative, building excitement and reinforcing that this wasn't just a tool—it was a strategic weapon.

## RESULT: Execution That Drove Results

The ZSI rollout was a **breakthrough success.** Sales reps were energized, better equipped, and more confident in the field. The combination of purpose, clarity, ownership, and tools led to extraordinary performance.

We not only **converted more than our target of five competitive surgeons,** but we also **exceeded our goal of 10% revenue growth above the market.**

It was a textbook example of how strategy, when executed with precision and belief, becomes unstoppable. Below is the Strategic Planning Canvas for this example.

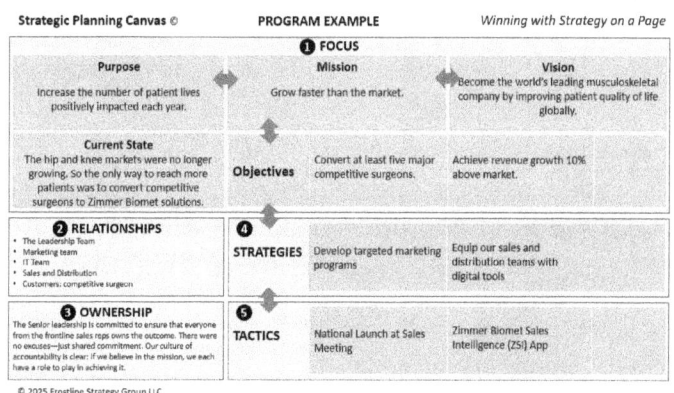

Strategic Planning Canvas for a Program

## Real-World Strategy in Action: A Non-Profit Example in Education

Strategy isn't just for business—it's essential for any organization with a mission, including non-profits. One powerful example comes from the field of education.

I had the honor of serving on the Board of School Trustees for the Lakeland School Corporation for eight years, including two as Board President. Lakeland had a proud history of academic performance and a dedicated team of educators. But by the time I joined the board, shifting demographics and changing community needs had taken a toll. The school system was beginning to fall behind in standardized test scores, and we knew something had to change.

We set out to create a focused strategy to turn things around.

- **Purpose:** Create future leaders through excellence in education.
- **Mission:** Improve the learning experience to drive measurable gains in standardized test performance.
- **Vision:** Become a top-performing school corporation in the state and the school of choice within our county.
- **Current State:** Academic performance was average and trending downward.
- **Objectives:** Improve standardized test scores by 10% annually and become a recognized school of choice.

### Relationships: Engage the Whole System

Success depended on alignment across all stakeholders:

- The School Board
- Teachers and school administrators

- Union leadership
- Most importantly, the students themselves

**Ownership: Build a Culture of Commitment**

We made it a priority to involve everyone—from faculty to students—in planning and implementation. When people are part of the process, they take ownership of the outcomes.

**Strategy: Redesign the System for Success**

We built our strategy on three pillars:

1. **Innovative learning models** that focused on true comprehension rather than teaching to the test.
2. **Tailored graduation tracks**, including an advanced honors track and a technical education track, to better serve students' diverse aspirations.
3. **Curriculum enhancements**, including materials aligned with standardized testing and training on test-taking skills.

**Tactics: Translate Strategy into Action**

Execution came through practical, high-impact actions:

- We engaged students and staff by always answering the question: *What's in it for me?*
- We assigned program leaders and cross-functional teams to drive each strategic initiative.
- We implemented clear metrics and leading indicators, including regular practice tests to monitor progress and adjust in real time.

**Results: Turning Vision into Reality**

The results spoke for themselves. We exceeded our 10% annual improvement goal and, within a few years, earned recognition as a 4-Star School and a Best Buy School by the Indiana Department of Education. Our story of transformation was even featured at the Indiana School Boards Association conference in Indianapolis.

This example proves that strategy—when it's focused, inclusive, and executed with discipline—can transform even the most challenged systems. Whether you're running a business, a non-profit, or a school, the principles are the same: align around a mission, build ownership, choose the right strategies, and make winning the only option.

**Real-World Strategy in Action: Turning a Personal Goal into a Personal Win**

Not every strategy plays out in a boardroom. Sometimes, the most important transformations begin in the mirror.

A few years ago, I set a simple, personal mission: **to lose weight and improve my health.** I wasn't training for a marathon or trying to reach some milestone number on a scale. I just wanted to feel better, think clearer, and take back control of my energy.

And just like in business, I knew that desire wasn't enough. I needed a strategy—and the discipline to follow through.

**Focus: Define the Mission and the Why**

My mission was clear: **lose weight and reclaim my health.** But the real fuel came from the *why*. I wanted to have more energy for my family, to feel strong again, to set an example of commitment. That purpose gave me the emotional clarity to stay grounded when motivation faded.

I set one measurable objective:

- **Lose 20 pounds in 90 days** by creating a consistent calorie deficit.

**Strategy: Choose the Right How**

Once the mission and objective were clear, the strategy came into focus:

- **Follow a simple diet and exercise plan** that fit my lifestyle and didn't rely on extremes.
- **Make sustainable changes** instead of quick-fix gimmicks.

I wasn't trying to become a nutritionist or a professional athlete. I just needed a plan that would create consistent results—and fit into the rhythm of my life.

**Tactics: Track. Limit. Move. Repeat.**

Here's where the rubber met the road.

- **Track calories daily,** using an app that gave me visibility into what I was really consuming.
- **Limit intake** to create a daily caloric deficit—no more mindless snacking or second helpings.
- **Burn calories through consistent exercise,** including early morning workouts and evening walks.
- **Review weekly progress,** and adjust as needed.

This part wasn't glamorous. But it was essential. I had to say no to dessert, yes to early alarms, and stay consistent—even when the scale wasn't moving. That's where belief and commitment came in.

Because here's the truth:

It doesn't matter how smart your strategy is, or how well-designed your tactics are—**if you don't follow through, nothing changes.**

You still have to order the salad. You still have to lace up your shoes. You still have to show up for yourself, every single day.

**Strategy Realization: How It Worked**

And that's what I did. Day by day, week by week. Not perfectly, but consistently.

- I tracked my numbers.
- I honored the plan.
- I stayed connected to the *why*.

And the weight started to come off. Slowly at first, then steadily. By the end of the 90 days, I had hit my goal. More importantly, I had built momentum—and proven to myself that I could do hard things with discipline and intention.

**Cause and Effect, Heart and Mind**

The logic was straightforward:

If I executed the **tactics** (track, limit, move),
Then I followed the **strategy** (diet + exercise),
Which helped me hit my **objective** (caloric deficit + consistency),
Which fulfilled my **mission** (lose weight),
Which reconnected me to my **purpose** (health, energy, example).
But beneath the logic was something deeper: **belief.** I believed it could work. I believed I could change. And that belief gave me the commitment to push through every resistance point along the way.

This is the power of personal strategy.

When the heart and mind are aligned, and the system is in place, **winning becomes a pattern—not just an outcome.**

Chapter 8 Summary

- **Belief is the ultimate multiplier.** Winning requires not just the right strategy, but the right mindset. Belief—combined with discipline, alignment, and structure—turns plans into action.

- **Cause-and-effect clarity drives results.** Strategy realization works like a chain:

    o Execute the **tactics,** deliver the **strategies**

    o Deliver the strategies, achieve the **objectives**

    o Achieve the objectives, fulfill the **mission**

    o Fulfill the mission, realize the **purpose and vision**

- **Structure creates momentum.** A cascading system keeps everything aligned and manageable.

- **Examples across contexts show the system in action:**
    o **Business:** Wolfpack Chassis proved how clarity, culture, and execution built a successful company from the ground up.
    o **Corporate:** Zimmer Biomet's sales conversion initiative demonstrated how belief, alignment, and tools transformed a stagnant market into growth.
    o **Non-Profit:** Lakeland Schools used the framework to improve academic performance and become a top-rated district.

- **Personal:** A health transformation showed how purpose, strategy, and discipline work at the individual level.

- **Execution is engineered, not accidental.** Success happens when every tactic supports a strategy, every strategy advances an objective, and every objective serves the mission.

- **The formula works everywhere.** Whether in boardrooms, classrooms, nonprofits, or personal lives, the combination of purpose, belief, alignment, and disciplined execution makes winning the only option

## Chapter 9

## A Passion for Winning

*"There are two kinds of organizations: those that are getting better, and those that are dying."*
— *Dr. W. Edwards Deming*

From the very beginning of my career—as an engineer designing industrial robots and medical devices—I've been driven by a single obsession: a relentless pursuit of better. I hold a medical device patent, and I still remember the thrill of seeing something go from a concept on paper to a physical product improving lives. That's where my love for innovation took root.

It was also where I first learned that winning isn't an event—it's a process. And that process demands a combination of creativity, rigor, and the courage to challenge the status quo.

My background in engineering, combined with Six Sigma training, shaped how I approached every problem—with curiosity, discipline, and a deep belief that there's always a better way. But as I transitioned into management and executive roles, I realized that technical skills weren't enough. To drive enduring success, you need something more foundational: a passion for strategy.

**Strategy as the Engine of Renewal**

That realization deepened when I returned to graduate school to earn my MBA at Indiana Tech. During a business strategy course, my professor introduced a concept that shows up in nearly every business textbook—the life-cycle curve: introduction, growth, maturity, and decline.

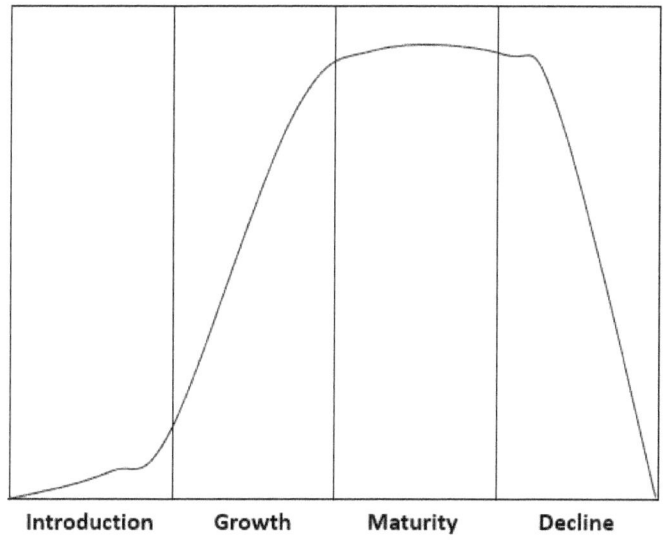

Business Life-Cycle Curve

At first glance, it looked like a natural progression, almost like the aging process. But I couldn't help asking the obvious question:

Why does every business model end in decline?

My professor responded with a simple but powerful insight:

"Because the world changes, and most organizations don't."

Technologies shift. Markets evolve. New entrants disrupt. And the companies that once dominated—household names like Kodak, Blockbuster, Blackberry—fade because they become comfortable with the way things are. They stop improving.

And then he said something that stuck with me:

"That's where strategy comes in. That's how you jump the curve."

## Jumping the Curve

The best companies don't ride the life-cycle curve to its end. They reinvent. They anticipate change—and create it. They move from decline back to growth by innovating new models, launching new offerings, or reimagining their purpose. That's what my professor called "jumping the curve."

That moment at the Cunningham Business Center sparked an idea that became a cornerstone of how I approach my work. I saw that the real winners—individuals and organizations—never wait for disruption to overtake them. They build a habit of strategic reinvention. They refuse to settle for past success. They view every challenge as a chance to sharpen their focus, evolve their strategy, and reignite their mission.

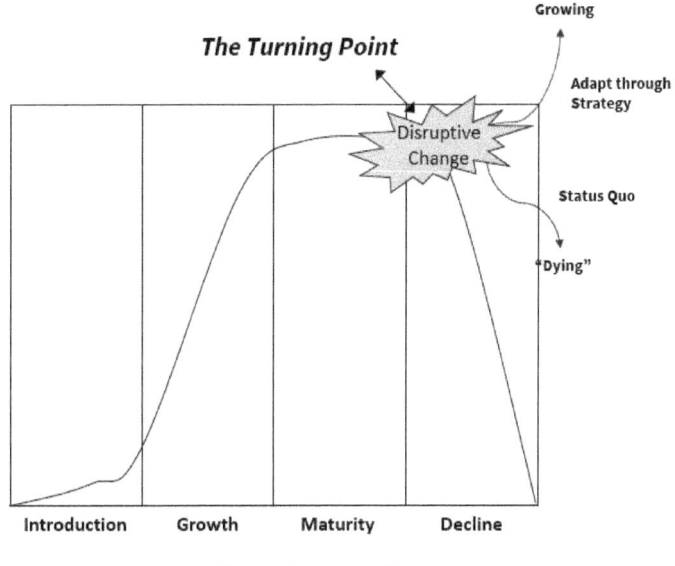

Jumping the Curve

This concept also echoes Eli Goldratt's principle from *The Goal*: the process of ongoing improvement. Not just incremental improvement, but continuous, intentional adaptation that fuels sustainable success.

### Strategy as a Lifelong Habit

I've used this mindset—and the strategic framework outlined in this book—as the foundation of my own journey:

- To start and grow a multi-million-dollar business from scratch
- To lead global teams through complex transformations

- To develop world-class systems and processes that create real, measurable value

But more than any of the titles or outcomes, it's the mindset that matters. The belief that we're either getting better or falling behind. There is no standing still.

The organizations that win over time are the ones that treat strategy as a living system—not a once-a-year exercise. They align purpose with action. They push for clarity. They empower their people. And they never stop learning.

That is what it means to have a passion for winning.

### The Discipline of Continuous Improvement

Winners don't rise by accident. They rise because they've built habits of progress—disciplined, deliberate, and sustained. That's the essence of **continuous improvement**, and it's the difference between fleeting success and enduring greatness.

*"Winners don't rise by accident. They rise because they've built habits of progress— disciplined, deliberate, and sustained."*

Throughout my career, I've seen organizations achieve extraordinary results—not because they had better resources or the perfect plan—but because they made **getting better a daily discipline.**

In engineering and operations, I learned the power of tools like **PDCA (Plan-Do-Check-Act)**, **Kaizen**, and **Six Sigma**. These weren't just technical tools—they were cultural mindsets. They taught me that improvement doesn't come in big, flashy leaps. It comes from doing the small things right, over and over, and having the humility to ask, *"How can this be better?"*

In fact, I've found that the organizations and leaders who are most committed to improvement are the ones who are *least* satisfied with yesterday's success. They build a culture where excellence is never assumed—it's pursued.

### Small Wins, Big Momentum

When we implemented the FROST framework across program teams at Zimmer Biomet, one of the most important shifts wasn't in the tools—it was in the *thinking*. We stopped looking at project delivery as a one-time push for results, and started treating it like an **evolving system**.

Each week, we reviewed leading indicators, addressed issues early, and asked tough questions—not to criticize, but to learn. And when a team found a better way, we documented it, shared it, and scaled it.

The improvements were often incremental:

- A clearer dashboard.
- A more proactive risk log.
- A smoother handoff between functions.

But the effect was exponential. Week by week, we built momentum. And momentum is one of the most underrated forces in strategy execution—it's what transforms effort into performance, and performance into competitive advantage.

### From Good Ideas to Great Systems

Many companies have good ideas. But few turn those ideas into *systems*—repeatable, measurable processes that deliver results at scale.

The FROST framework provides that structure. By aligning **focus, relationships, and ownership** with the right strategies and tactics, it creates a system where improvement isn't just possible—it's expected.

And when improvement becomes part of the culture, the organization moves from reactive to proactive. From complacent to committed. From good to great.

**Building a Culture of Strategic Curiosity**

"The important thing is not to stop questioning. Curiosity has its own reason for existing."
—Albert Einstein

Behind every great strategy is a question someone was bold enough to ask. And behind every enduring organization is a culture where those questions aren't just tolerated—they're encouraged, expected, and acted upon.

Strategic curiosity isn't about chasing shiny objects. It's not reactive brainstorming or innovation for innovation's sake. It's about **disciplined thinking**—a hunger to understand the *why*, the *what if*, and the *what's next* behind every decision, trend, and outcome. It's the mindset that constantly searches for deeper clarity, sharper insight, and better answers.

In my experience, organizations that win consistently are the ones that embed this kind of thinking deep into their DNA.

They ask questions like:

- Is this still the right mission?
- Are our strategies still aligned with what's changed?
- What are we missing?
- What would disrupt us tomorrow?
- What problem are we really trying to solve?

They don't wait for disruption to force reinvention. They pursue reinvention because **they know that stagnation is the silent killer of greatness.**

## Curiosity as a Strategic Advantage

One of the most powerful questions I've learned to ask is deceptively simple:

What needs to be true for this to succeed?

It's a question that cuts through assumptions and exposes risks, constraints, and blind spots. It invites the team to imagine future obstacles and proactively solve them before they appear. It shifts the focus from guessing outcomes to engineering success.

Strategic curiosity also fuels innovation. Some of the best ideas I've seen didn't come from senior leadership—they came from someone on the front lines who saw something others didn't, and had the courage (and psychological safety) to ask:

Why do we do it this way? What if we tried something different?

Curiosity opens the door for contribution. And contribution drives ownership.

## Leading with Questions, Not Just Answers

As leaders, we sometimes feel the pressure to have all the answers. But in reality, great leadership often starts with asking better questions.

Peter Drucker once said:

"The most serious mistakes are not being made as a result of wrong answers. The true dangerous thing is asking the wrong question."

In my own leadership journey, I've found that the more I lead with curiosity, the more engaged and committed the team becomes. When people feel like their perspectives matter, when their insights are sought—not just received—they step up. They think deeper. They take ownership.

This is what separates good teams from great ones: not intelligence or talent alone, but the presence of a culture where learning is continuous and questioning is safe.

### Curiosity in the FROST Framework

Strategic curiosity is embedded throughout the FROST framework:

- In **Focus**, we ask what truly matters—and what doesn't.
- In **Relationships**, we seek to understand others' perspectives, values, and motivations.
- In **Ownership**, we empower individuals to question and improve what they own.
- In **Strategy**, we challenge assumptions and test scenarios.
- In **Tactics**, we refine the plan with feedback and iteration.

Every stage becomes a chance to learn, adapt, and improve.

### Final Thought: Curiosity as the Antidote to Complacency

Curiosity isn't just a spark of creativity. It's the antidote to complacency. When strategy becomes a living, breathing conversation—fueled by questions, not just answers—it creates a culture that's agile, resilient, and always evolving.

Because in the end, the most dangerous phrase in business is:

"This is how we've always done it."

And the most powerful response?

"What if we could do it better?"

## Chapter 9 Summary

- **Winning Is a Process, Not an Event.** Success demands creativity, rigor, and the courage to challenge the status quo. Strategy and innovation are the engines that sustain progress over time.

- **Jumping the Curve.** Businesses fail when they stop adapting (e.g., Kodak, Blockbuster). Winners "jump the curve" by reinventing themselves before disruption overtakes them. Strategy enables organizations to move from decline back to growth.

- **Continuous Improvement as a Discipline.** Tools like PDCA, Kaizen, and Six Sigma aren't just methods—they're cultural mindsets. Progress is built through small, consistent improvements that create exponential momentum. Momentum, fueled by small wins, becomes a competitive advantage.

- **Systems Over Ideas.** Many companies have good ideas; few turn them into repeatable, measurable systems. The FROST framework creates the structure to make improvement a cultural expectation.

- **Strategic Curiosity as a Habit.** Winners ask bold, forward-looking questions: Is this still the right mission? What's next? What are we missing? Curiosity isn't reactive—it's disciplined thinking that prevents complacency. The most powerful question: What needs to be true for this to succeed?

- **Leadership Through Questions.** Great leaders don't have all the answers—they ask better questions. Cultures that encourage questioning foster ownership, innovation, and resilience.

- **Curiosity Embedded in FROST**
    - **Focus:** Ask what truly matters.
    - **Relationships:** Understand perspectives and motivations.
    - **Ownership:** Encourage improvement in what people own.
    - **Strategy:** Challenge assumptions and test scenarios.
    - **Tactics:** Adapt with feedback and iteration.

## Chapter 10

## Make Winning Your Habit

*"People do not decide their futures. They decide their habits, and their habits decide their futures."*
— *F. M. Alexander*

You've made it this far because something inside you believes there's a better way—a better way to lead, to plan, to execute, to live. That belief is the beginning of transformation. But belief alone isn't enough. It must be followed by focus, fueled by purpose, executed with discipline, and sustained through action.

The truth is, **strategy is not a once-a-year event.** It's not a document that collects dust or a slide deck lost in an inbox. **Strategy is a living system.** It is how you move with intention, how you align what matters, how you bring people together to create something bigger than themselves.

In this book, you've learned a framework for making that happen—a system for turning ideas into action and goals into reality:

- **Focus** gives you clarity of purpose—defining your mission, vision, and measurable objectives.
- **Relationships** ensure you can build, align, and mobilize the team that will get you there.
- **Ownership** turns passive agreement into active commitment—creating a culture of accountability and belief.
- **Strategy** provides the "how"—the critical paths that will move you toward your goals.
- **Tactics** bring the strategy to life—step by step, day by day, decision by decision.

Together, these elements form the **FROST Strategy Pyramid™**, supported by the **Strategic Planning Canvas**—tools not just to think differently, but to act differently.

**Winning Is a Process**

If you've followed along, you now have everything you need to win—with clarity, with conviction, and with discipline. The rest is up to you.

The most successful people and organizations aren't lucky. They're intentional. They put in the work. They embrace the process. And most importantly, **they never stop getting better.**

They don't win once.
**They make winning a habit.**

**Strategy Is for Everyone**

If there's one thing I hope you take away from this book, it's this: **strategy isn't just for the boardroom.**

It's for the business owner launching their next product.
It's for the nonprofit leader transforming a community.
It's for the frontline manager trying to inspire a team.
It's for the individual who wants to live with more purpose and impact.

Strategy is for anyone who wants to win—not by chance, but by design.

**The Next Step Is Yours**

So ask yourself:

- What mission are you ready to commit to?
- What vision are you ready to pursue?
- What change are you ready to lead?

Because nothing happens until something moves. And nothing moves until *you* do.

> *"If there's one thing I hope you take away from this book, it's this: strategy isn't just for the boardroom. Strategy is for anyone who wants to win—not by chance, but by design."*

The future doesn't belong to the status quo. It belongs to the curious, the committed, and the courageous. The ones who are bold enough to set a vision, align a team, own the outcome, and take action.

It belongs to those who are ready to win—with strategy.

Remember - you can accomplish anything with the right strategy, and life's a lot more fun when you're winning.

Let's get to work.

## Chapter 10 Summary

- **Belief Is the Beginning.** Transformation starts with belief in a better way—but belief alone is not enough. Winning requires focus, purpose, discipline, and sustained action.

- **Strategy Is a Living System.** Strategy isn't a once-a-year plan or a dusty document—it's a way of moving with intention. It aligns what matters, brings people together, and turns ideas into reality.

- **The FROST Framework in Action**
    - **Focus:** Clarity of mission, vision, and objectives.
    - **Relationships:** Build trust, alignment, and collaboration.
    - **Ownership:** Create accountability and belief across the team.
    - **Strategy:** Choose the right paths forward with discipline.
    - **Tactics:** Execute consistently—decision by decision, day by day.
    - Together, the FROST Pyramid™ and Strategic Planning Canvas provide a practical system for results.

- **Winning Is a Habit.** Success isn't luck—it's intentional. The best people and organizations win by embracing the process and never stopping their pursuit of better.

- **Strategy Is for Everyone.** Not limited to boardrooms or executives. Equally powerful for entrepreneurs, nonprofits, frontline leaders, and individuals pursuing personal goals.
- **The Call to Action**
    - Ask yourself:
        - What mission am I ready to commit to?
        - What vision am I ready to pursue?
        - What change am I ready to lead?
    - The future belongs to those who are curious, committed, and courageous enough to act.

Winning with strategy is about more than plans—it's about people, purpose, and progress. When you combine belief with discipline, align focus with action, and create ownership at every level, winning stops being an accident and starts being a way of life. And in the end, remember this: you can accomplish anything with the right strategy—and life's a lot more fun when you're winning.

# Appendix

## How to Use the Strategic Planning Canvas

### A One-Page Framework for Strategic Clarity and Execution

The **Strategic Planning Canvas** is a powerful tool designed to bring the FROST Strategy Pyramid™ to life on a single page. It serves as both a **planning tool** and a **communication tool**—clarifying purpose, aligning teams, and turning strategic intent into meaningful action.

Whether you're a CEO leading a company, a team leader planning next quarter, or an individual pursuing a personal goal, the Strategic Planning Canvas helps you stay focused, aligned, and accountable.

◇ **Purpose of the Strategic Planning Canvas**

The Strategic Planning Canvas distills everything into one actionable view:

- It connects your **Purpose, Mission,** and **Vision** to the **Objectives, Strategies,** and **Tactics** that will bring them to life.
- It builds in **Relationships** and **Ownership** as core enablers of execution.
- It becomes a living document to track progress, identify gaps, and communicate direction.

❋ **Before You Begin: Prepare for a Strategic Planning Session**

To make the most of the Strategic Planning Canvas, begin with a structured strategic planning session. Here's how to prepare:

- **Invite the right people:** Bring together a cross-functional group of key stakeholders who understand the mission and will be involved in execution.
- **Set the tone:** Share the FROST framework and let the team know this is a working session to clarify focus, align priorities, and build commitment.
- **Create space:** Use a whiteboard, digital collaboration tool, or large printed version of the Strategic Planning Canvas.

## 🛠 Step-by-Step: How to Complete the Strategic Planning Canvas

### 1. FOCUS

This is the foundation of your strategy. Complete this section first.

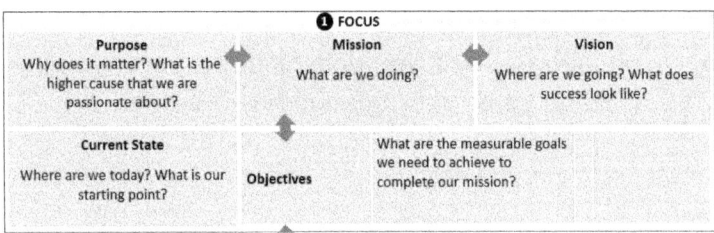

- **Purpose (Why you exist):**
  Why do we do what we do? What impact are we trying to create?
  *(e.g., "To improve the quality of life for patients around the world.")*

  > **Purpose**
  > Why does it matter? What is the higher cause that we are passionate about?

- **Mission (What you do):**
  What do we do every day to fulfill our purpose?
  *(e.g., "Develop and deliver innovative orthopedic solutions.")*

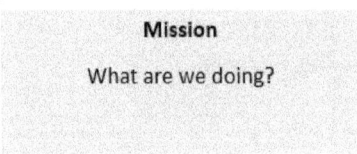

- **Vision (What success looks like):**
  Where are we headed? What does winning look like in the future?
  *(e.g., "To be the global leader in musculoskeletal innovation and outcomes.")*

  > **Vision**
  > Where are we going? What does success look like?

- **Current State (Where we are today):**
  A brief honest summary of your current situation, challenges, or performance.

  > **Current State**
  > Where are we today? What is our starting point?

- **Objectives (What must be achieved):**
  Objectives close the gap between where you are (current state) and where you want to be (vision). These should be SMART (Specific, Measurable, Achievable, Relevant, Time-bound).
  *(e.g., "Grow revenue by 15% in the next 12 months.")*

  > **Objectives** — What are the measurable goals we need to achieve to complete our mission?

---

## 2. RELATIONSHIPS

This section ensures that you have the right people, alignment, and culture to succeed.

- **Key Stakeholders / Team Members:**

Who must be involved for this strategy to succeed?
- **Trusted Relationships:**
Where do we need to build trust or alignment to move forward?
- **Influence Strategy:**
How will we build buy-in? How will we communicate across the organization?

> **❷ RELATIONSHIPS**
> Who is critical to success? How will we build trust and shared commitment?

## 3. OWNERSHIP

Clarify accountability and commitment.

- **Leadership Commitment:**
Who is ultimately accountable for achieving each objective?
- **Individual Ownership:**
Who owns each strategy or tactic? Are roles and expectations clear?
- **Cultural Expectations:**
What values or behaviors will we promote to support execution?
*(e.g., "No blame, no excuses—only solutions and results.")*

> **❸ OWNERSHIP**
> Who is responsible and accountable for what? Are the owners aligned and committed?

## 4. STRATEGIES

Define your big "how"—the major initiatives or programs that will help you achieve the objectives.

- For each **Objective**, ask:

"What strategic initiative will best move us toward this goal?"

- These should be directional, not overly detailed. (e.g., "Expand into adjacent markets" or "Launch digital transformation program.")

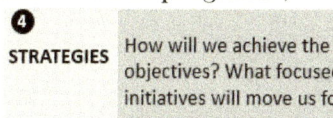

**STRATEGIES** — How will we achieve the objectives? What focused initiatives will move us forward?

## 5. TACTICS

The specific actions or workstreams that will bring each strategy to life.

- Break down each **Strategy** into actionable steps. (e.g., "Conduct competitive analysis," "Launch customer pilot," "Hire digital lead.")
- Use a **RAID log** or **Action Tracker** in conjunction with this section to monitor issues, risks, and dependencies.

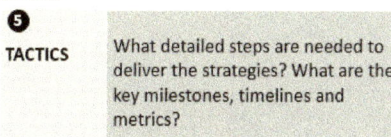

**TACTICS** — What detailed steps are needed to deliver the strategies? What are the key milestones, timelines and metrics?

## How to Use the Canvas in Ongoing Strategy Realization

Once completed, the Strategic Planning Canvas should serve as a **living document** that you refer to regularly. Here's how:

### As a Strategic Compass

- Revisit the canvas at the start of every team meeting or planning session.
- Ensure all actions are connected to the bigger picture.

### For Quarterly Reviews

- Evaluate what's on track, what's off-track, and what needs to change.
- Refresh tactics as strategies evolve.

### To Facilitate Alignment

- Use the canvas to onboard new team members or align cross-functional partners.
- Keep everyone focused on what matters most.

### As a Storytelling Tool

- Translate strategic complexity into a clear narrative.
- Share progress with executives, stakeholders, and even customers or partners.

## Final Word

Completing your Strategic Planning Canvas is not the end of the journey—it's the beginning. It's your playbook, your compass, your commitment. Keep it visible. Keep it current. Keep it alive.

As covered in chapter 7, the Strategic Planning Canvas should also be used across departments and teams to drive alignment and commitment as shown in the business example below.

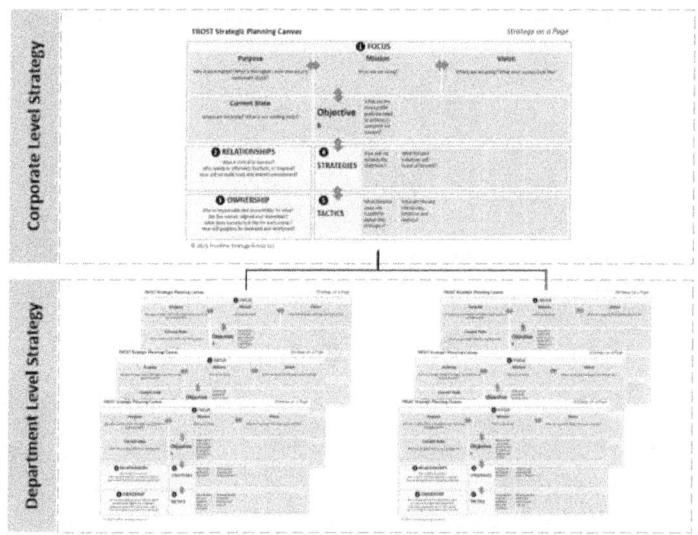

**Cascading the Strategic Planning Canvas to Drive Alignment and Commitment**

When used with discipline, this tool becomes more than a worksheet. It becomes your **roadmap to winning**—with clarity, conviction, and purpose.

# Strategic Planning Canvas™

*Strategy on a Page*

## ❶ FOCUS

**Purpose**
Why does it matter? What is the higher cause that we are passionate about?

**Mission**
What are we doing?

**Vision**
Where are we going? What does success look like?

**Current State**
Where are we today? What is our starting point?

**Objectives**
What are the measurable goals we need to achieve to complete our mission?

## ❷ RELATIONSHIPS
Who is critical to success? How will we build trust and shared commitment?

## ❹ STRATEGIES
How will we achieve the objectives? What focused initiatives will move us forward?

## ❸ OWNERSHIP
Who is responsible and accountable for what? Are the owners aligned and committed?

## ❺ TACTICS
What detailed steps are needed to deliver the strategies? What are the key milestones, timelines and metrics?

© 2025 Frostline Strategy Group LLC

## About The Author

*"The best way out is always through."*
— Robert Frost, American Poet

Robert Frost is a visionary strategist and transformation leader with over 20 years of experience guiding organizations—from Fortune 500 giants like Medtronic and Zimmer Biomet to private equity-backed startups, mid-market challengers, and non-profits —through bold growth and reinvention. As the founding President, CEO, and Chairman of the Board of Wolfpack Chassis and now President and Managing Director of Frostline Strategy Group, Robert has dedicated his career to helping companies unlock their full potential through disciplined strategy and inspired execution.

With an MBA from Indiana Tech and undergraduate degrees in both engineering and business administration, Robert combines technical rigor with business insight. He is a certified Project Management Professional (PMP), Six Sigma Green Belt, and Prosci-certified change practitioner. Robert is also a former faculty member and advisory board member for the Indiana Tech School of Business.

Above all, Robert is passionate about leveraging strategy to help leaders and teams build winning organizations—ones that embrace purpose, outthink the competition, and deliver lasting impact. A dynamic speaker and mentor, he is committed to sharing the transformative power of strategy as a force for growth, excellence, and enduring success. Robert can be contacted at info@frostlinestrategygroup.com.

www.ingramcontent.com/pod-product-compliance
Lightning Source LLC
Chambersburg PA
CBHW032136040426
42449CB00005B/262